PROPOSAL
WRITING

5
EDITION

To Ron Coley, my husband, who supported me in all stages of this book; and who had faith when I faltered, praise and inspiration when I doubted, and love and friendship always. —S. C.

To my granddaughter, Maya, and grandson, Kai, who inspire great hope for a beautiful future. —C. S.

PROPOSAL WRITING

5 EDITION

Effective Grantsmanship for Funding

Soraya M. Coley, Ph.D.
President
California State Polytechnic University, Pomona

Cynthia A. Scheinberg, Ph.D.
Private Practice

Los Angeles | London | New Delhi
Singapore | Washington DC | Melbourne

FOR INFORMATION:

SAGE Publications, Inc.
2455 Teller Road
Thousand Oaks, California 91320
E-mail: order@sagepub.com

SAGE Publications Ltd.
1 Oliver's Yard
55 City Road
London, EC1Y 1SP
United Kingdom

SAGE Publications India Pvt. Ltd.
B 1/I 1 Mohan Cooperative Industrial Area
Mathura Road, New Delhi 110 044
India

SAGE Publications Asia-Pacific Pte. Ltd.
3 Church Street
#10-04 Samsung Hub
Singapore 049483

Acquisitions Editor: Nathan Davidson
eLearning Editor: Morgan Shannon
Production Editor: Tracy Buyan
Copy Editor: Tammy Giesmann
Typesetter: Hurix Systems Pvt. Ltd.
Proofreader: Laura Webb
Indexer: Teddy Diggs
Cover Designer: Anupama Krishnan
Marketing Manager: Shari Countryman

Printed in the United States of America

Library of Congress Cataloging-in-Publication Data

Names: Coley, Soraya M. (Soraya Moore), author. | Scheinberg, Cynthia A., author.

Title: Proposal writing : effective grantsmanship for funding / Soraya M. Coley, Cynthia A. Scheinberg.

Description: Fifth edition. | Thousand Oaks, California: SAGE, [2017] | Includes bibliographical references and index.

Identifiers: LCCN 2016017161 | ISBN 9781483376431 (pbk. : alk. paper)

Subjects: LCSH: Proposal writing in human services. | Social service.

Classification: LCC HV41 .C548 2017 | DDC 658.15/224–dc23 LC record available at https://lccn.loc.gov/2016017161

This book is printed on acid-free paper.

SUSTAINABLE FORESTRY INITIATIVE
Certified Chain of Custody
Promoting Sustainable Forestry
www.sfiprogram.org
SFI-01268
SFI label applies to text stock

16 17 18 19 20 10 9 8 7 6 5 4 3 2 1

Brief Contents

Detailed Contents

Preface

We are pleased to offer this fifth edition of *Proposal Writing* that substantially updates the materials while broadening the appeal of the book to health, education, social services, and human services providers. We have increased the size of the book by two chapters and two additional appendices (40 pages total). As before, we have kept the book jargon-free.

The first four chapters of the book orient the reader to the field of grant writing: the history of philanthropy, nonprofit organizations and their purposes, sources of funding and application processes, and an overview of the contents of a proposal. This structure will allow the user (or teacher) the flexibility of viewing these foundational materials separately and as needed.

Chapter 5 is a transitional chapter that orients the reader to the task of writing the proposal and addresses the unique writing challenges when a proposal is developed within an established organization (that has a history and proven track record of providing successful services) versus writing for a new organization. This chapter also addresses the unique demands of writing a joint, collaborative proposal.

Chapters 6–11 take the reader through the rigorous process of grant writing. Starting with program development through a step-by-step process that includes looking at demographic and research data to determine the need for the program. Addressing community readiness and barriers to services as well as program sustainability is discussed.

The reader is taken from program design into a very comprehensive crash course on program evaluation. Readers will learn why it is important to measure program outcomes, how to measure them, and how to plan an evaluation design early in the planning process. After this, the reader will learn how to refine program ideas into objectives and implementation activities and write them in a format demanded by various funders.

In most applications, the program description or need statement is the heart of the proposal. The book provides the reader with a template upon which to develop and sketch out a compelling narrative to accurately represent and *sell* the project idea to the funder. The last two chapters address budgeting and budget justifications, subcontracting, and contract negotiations. More sample proposal sections are included in the final chapter and a sample memorandum of understanding.

We are grateful for the book's success and indebted to many people who have had a hand in improving this edition. The book reflects the input of faculty, students, and community agency members who have used the book in the teaching and writing of grants. We have created a book that integrates their recommendations with our own experiences resulting in an effective guide to grant writing.

We thank our new editor at SAGE, Nathan Davidson, and previous editor Kassie Graves, along with Carrie Montoya, formerly Senior Editorial Assistant for Human Services. We are indebted to outside readers who provided us with their thoughtful feedback including: Joyce Weil, University of Northern Colorado, Gerontology Department; Rebecca L. Thomas, University of Connecticut, School of Social Work; Richard Hoefer, University of Texas at Arlington, Social Work; Adrian S. Petrescu, Bellevue University, MPA Program; Brian Nerney, Metropolitan State University; Christine Hempowicz, University of Bridgeport; James Wolff, Boston University, School of Public Health; Richard Mushi, PhD, Mississippi Valley State University; and Sandra Pavelka, Florida Gulf Coast University. We also thank Lietta Wood for reading and editing early versions of this manuscript. Finally, we invite you, our reader, to contact us with any thoughts or suggestions you have to improve this book at proposalwriting5thed@gmail.com.

1

An Orientation to Proposal Writing

A Book for the Beginning Grant Writer

There is nothing more exciting or gratifying than to participate in designing a program, writing a proposal that gets funded, and, ultimately, seeing that program come to life in the community! This book is written to help you, the beginning grant writer, understand the basics of grant writing and develop the necessary skills to write an acceptable, and hopefully successful, grant application. We avoid the use of technical jargon as much as possible and provide a step-by-step process to help you write a proposal for a nonprofit organization (including schools) seeking public funding through governmental or private funders. (For those of you writing research proposals, we recommend: *The Nuts and Bolts of Grant Writing* by Cynthia E. Carr [2015] and *Writing Successful Grant Proposals* by Robert J. Sternberg [2014].)

Grant writing is often the primary means by which a nonprofit funds its programs and services. Whether you are a person in a club or association, an employee in an agency asked to step up and write a grant, or a student taking a grant writing course, you will be challenged to enter into an open-minded, critical thinking process that will lead to a completed proposal. In this process you will be asked to

- identify and state issues clearly and succinctly,
- understand and apply research findings to program design,
- design effective program evaluation to measure the impact of the program,
- create and justify a budget for the project, and
- fit this within a predetermined number of pages and format.

Once you have learned how to write a state or federal proposal as outlined in this book you will be able to tackle just about any proposal that comes your way. Plus, you will find that these skills will help make you a more desirable employee in the nonprofit sector or lead to a career as a freelance grant writer taking on projects for a variety of agencies. (For more information on a career in grant writing, you might want to consult with national organizations including the Association of Fundraising Professionals [AFP], the Grant Writers' Association, the Grant Professionals Association, or the American Grant Writers' Association. These associations help establish professional ethics and resources for grant writers, provide training and certification, and, in some cases, help individuals find quality jobs.) In all, there are many things you can do with these skills, and, we believe they are well worth learning.

We begin this journey with background information on the history of philanthropy and on nonprofit agencies, and then move directly into the business of writing grant applications and identifying funding for your program.

A Brief History of Giving and Philanthropy

The Latin word *philanthropy* is defined roughly as "love for mankind" (Dictionary.com, 2012). If you are working in the nonprofit sector, you are probably already aware that "love for mankind" can take many forms. Today, U.S. political orientations are on a continuum. One perspective encourages individuals to "pull themselves up by their own bootstraps" while the other seeks to provide a "hand up." Throughout U.S. history you will see the flow of giving surge and retreat based on the political party in power and their beliefs.

The history of giving in the United States has its roots in 16th-century Elizabethan Poor Laws of England that "were administered through parish overseers, who provided relief for the aged, sick, and infant poor, as well as work for the able-bodied in workhouses" ("Poor Law," 2012). Under the Poor Laws, persons who were needy through no fault of their own—such as the elderly, the sick, widows with children, and orphans—were cared for, while those who were needy but viewed to have caused their need, or perceived as being able to address their need without assistance, were fairly ignored. The ignored population included older children/young adults, pregnant single mothers, and criminals.

The Puritans followed the Elizabethan Poor Law model in caring for needy members in the community and took up collections in the parishes to meet those needs. Throughout much of U.S. history, benevolent associations were created as a kind of community-based insurance plan where individuals joined the association and paid dues that were used to help a family with illness or the costs of burial. These associations were established along the lines of ethnicity, employment, or religious affiliation.

The first grants made by the U.S. government were land grants providing the opportunity for citizens to obtain property upon which to build a home and put down roots. Bounty Land Warrants were provided to soldiers in the Revolutionary War in lieu of financial compensation. The Morrill Act of 1862 provided 30,000 acres of land for each congressional district that resulted in the creation of 69 colleges such as Cornell University and Massachusetts Institute of Technology.

The late 1800s and early 1900s marked a period of explosive growth in strategies to meet community needs. In 1889, Jane Addams founded Hull House, a settlement house that accepted needy men, women, and children, and provided a range of services on site and advocacy for improved schools and services. Jane Addams and Hull House mark the beginning of social work as a profession in the United States. The following quote illustrates the struggle that even well-established nonprofit agencies can have in obtaining consistent funding. In 2012, Hull House is forced to close:

> Jane Addams Hull House Association will be out of business Friday, leaving employees and clients scrambling to fill a void the 122-year-old organization will leave. Despite announcing last week plans to close in March, board Chairman Stephen Saunders said Wednesday that the organization will fold this

week because it can no longer afford to stay open. He also said Hull House plans to file Friday for bankruptcy. (Thayer, 2012)

In the early 1900s, the first foundations came into being: The Carnegie Foundation was founded in 1905 to promote education and is the foundation that developed and manages grants for higher education known as Pell Grants. Shortly thereafter, in response to a desire to do something good with his money, John D. Rockefeller, Sr., established the Rockefeller Foundation in 1913 with a mission to promote the well-being of humanity around the world. Just as these foundations were created out of the wealth of individuals, so it is today with individual, family, and corporate foundations created to give back to the community per the desire and specifications of the creator.

In 1913, the United States government began collecting income taxes and grants were made by the federal government to address critical needs and disasters. The country was well into the Great Depression in 1933 under Republican President Herbert Hoover. Hoover believed that the depression would eventually be resolved through legislation that supported businesses and, ultimately, when business was good, employees would receive the benefit in increased wages (this is called "trickle-down" economics). In March 1933, a Democratic president, Franklin Delano Roosevelt (FDR) was elected to office. FDR believed that the country needed more direct governmental intervention directed to the individual to end the Depression. Through two terms in office, he created a New Deal with numerous programs including the Social Security Administration (SSA), the Works Progress Administration (WPA), the Federal Deposit Insurance Corporation, the Securities and Exchange Commission, and the National Labor Relations Board. These social programs provided jobs for the unemployed, put food on the family table, and spurred the development of a robust infrastructure of roads, bridges, dams, and other public works.

The next burst of social programs came in the 1960s under Democratic President Lyndon B. Johnson's "Great Society" when there was a flurry of social programs, including those to address racial injustice and the "War on Poverty." The most recent surge in social programs was the American Recovery and Reinvestment Act (ARRA) signed by President Barack Obama to provide financial stimulus to the states hit hardest by the Great Recession. ARRA's primary purpose is to support social programs and to create jobs with $831 billion committed between 2009 and 2019.

As you can see, particular social issues come in and out of style and face reductions or increases in funding based on the politics of the day. There is true variability in the world of giving. The types of programs funded by Congress are subject to realignment and changes in the focus of politics.

Differences Between Grants and Contracts

In order to make some initial terms clear, the process of writing a proposal for funding has come to be known as *grant writing* and the individual(s) responsible for the writing of the proposal is a *grant writer*. The entity providing the money is called the *funder*. While it is commonly said that one writes a proposal to obtain a *grant*, it may be that the end result is actually a *contract*. Be that as it may, we will continue to follow the generally accepted convention and continue to use the word *grant* freely throughout this book.

Contracts for services, or *fee-for-service contracts* as they are often called, require the agency to provide services on behalf of a funder and the agency is reimbursed for services delivered. For example, a community dental clinic has successfully won a contract with the county to provide dental care to low-income children. The multi-page document (the contract) signed by the agency and the county will spell out the details of the services to be delivered. In this example, the contract states that the clinic is contracted to provide 100 units of amalgam filling at $30 per unit, 10 units of crown at $400 per unit, and 100 units of cleaning at $40 per unit. The clinic bills the county in arrears (after the delivery of services) of service provided. If the clinic does not need five of the 10 units of crowns in the contract, they will most likely need to make a modification of the contract or risk losing this amount from the contract. In general, a contract requires a great deal of management to insure that all services are delivered appropriately, services are billed and reimbursed appropriately, and timely changes are made to the contract to insure full use of the funds. (More on this topic in Chapter 10 under Other Budgeting Issues.)

On the other hand, we could imagine that this same clinic has also received a grant from the CSM Foundation, a corporate funder in the community. The terms of the corporate grant are that the agency will provide dental care to 100 low-income children. The grant does not quantify the type of care the children will receive, just that the funds will be used to serve 100 children. The agency will often receive the full amount of the grant at the beginning of the fiscal year and will report its progress to the foundation making sure to note the number of low-income children served.

It is generally true that grants are more flexible in terms of what they will fund and require less detailed accounting of services than contracts. For example, a federal funder such as the Department of Health Services will not reimburse a luncheon for clients, while a private foundation like the Bill and Melinda Gates Foundation might easily approve the request to celebrate a milestone in the program and request a brief report on the luncheon event.

The process of seeking funding for the nonprofit agency opens the door to a rich and fascinating funding world that may include tapping into the altruistic drives of individual donors, following the vagaries of politics to understand and tap into governmental funding, and seeking to develop partnerships to access the wealth and influence of private foundations. The proposal carries the expression of community need to the funder, and, if successful, results in a contract for services, a grant-in-aid, or, simply, a grant.

Request for Proposals (RFP)

There are grants and contracts available to fund educational, environmental, cultural, psychological, health and social programs, and services. Funding that comes through the government is known as *public* funding while funding that comes through a foundation or corporation is known as *private* funding. Public funds are available through federal, state, county, and city governments. Private funding is available through foundations that are created to raise and distribute funds called *community foundations* or those created by corporations to distribute some of their profits into the community, or simply those created by individuals to distribute their wealth through a family foundation.

In most cases, the funder announces that they have funds available to give by issuing a Request for Proposals (RFP). In some instances, you may see a Request for Applications (RFA), a Notice of Funding Announcements (NOFA), a Request for Quotes (RFQ), or other variations on that theme. The funder will often announce the availability of funds on their website, in newsletters, and through the mail. The RFP provides information as to the

- type of funding that is available,
- the target population,
- topics to be addressed and desired outcomes,
- eligibility to apply for the funding,
- the amount of funding allocated,
- the source of funding and funder's goals,
- the format of the submitted proposal (spacing, typeface, and font, etc.),
- a listing of all documents that should be attached in an appendix,
- a description of the review process and scoring procedure,

- the due date for receipt of the proposal, and
- links to any forms needed to prepare the proposal.

The first thing you should do with an RFP is *read it carefully*. Take time to make certain that the organization is eligible to apply for the funds, that the target population in the RFP matches the target population you want to serve, and that the timeline is acceptable and doable. Get out your high-lighter and mark the important information. The grant writer is responsible to know the details of the RFP down to the nitty-gritty of font size and spacing. Read and reread this document. (If you have not seen an RFP we recommend that you look online at Grants.gov or go to a specific federal agency to view a complete RFP package.)

2

Understanding the Nonprofit Agency

About the Nonprofit

With few exceptions, the nonprofit agency is the only business type that is eligible to obtain governmental grants and contracts. The nonprofit agency can be known by many names:

- Public charity
- Not-for-profit organization or agency
- Nongovernmental organization (NGO)
- Community-based organization (CBO)

A nonprofit agency is usually established in response or reaction to a particular community need or issue. In its most simple form, the agency is created by a group of citizens who gather together, agree certain services are needed, write a mission statement, create a board of directors and by-laws, and submit an application to the secretary of state and the Internal Revenue Service (IRS) for determination on their nonprofit status. According to the National Center for Charitable Statistics there are over 1.5 million registered charities (NCCS Quick Facts About Nonprofits (http://nccs.urban.org/statistics/quickfacts.cfm). Public benefit charities are the largest category with a total of 1,036,231 registered.

Since 1913, agencies that are established for public benefit receive a designation of 501(c)(3) through the IRS. This designation means that the agency is exempted from paying taxes on the revenue it earns and that "none of its earnings may inure to any private shareholder or individual" (Internal Revenue Service, 2016). There is a common misunderstanding that a non-profit organization cannot make a profit. It can, and if it is going to be a viable business, it must! This tax designation allows the agency to avoid taxation on its profits but it pays regular payroll taxes on employees, sales tax on purchases (except on products used in resale with a permit), sales tax on items sold, and in many cases, property taxes. A viable nonprofit agency develops ways to generate income that can be allocated into a reserve fund. Many agencies will strive to have about 10% of their annual budgets in reserve.

From the moment of its birth, the nonprofit agency is on a hunt for funds to enact its mission in the community. The following are some ways in which nonprofit agencies generate revenue:

- *Events* such as dinners, auctions, picnics, dances, or pledge drives to raise money
- *Donors,* or those individuals who contribute financially to the agency
- *Corporate donors* who give funds through a grant process
- *Products* the agency creates and then sells, such as educational brochures or booklets
- *Clients* who may contribute financially to the agency by paying a reduced fee-for-service
- *Businesses* the agency runs that further their mission and generate an income
- *Grants and contracts* from local government, state government, and/or federal governmental offices

Most social service agencies will receive the bulk of their income through grants and contracts with their annual budget looking somewhat like Figure 2.1.

Each source of potential funding has its own rules and expectations in relation to the type of programs it will fund, how it will receive requests for funding, and the style of the proposal or application it will accept. (Every agency determines its *fiscal year* which could be on a calendar year January

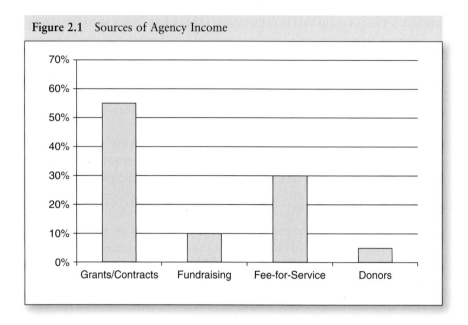

Figure 2.1   Sources of Agency Income

to December; on a state budget year, July 1 through June 30 of the following year; or a federal budget calendar, October 1 through September 30 of the following year. An agency receives funding in whatever fiscal year the funder has and prepares reports accordingly.)

Mission-Driven Analysis of the Agency/Organization

In most cases, when you receive an RFP, the funder has stated goals and objectives, or a rationale for funding, which articulates the type of outcomes wanted as a result of the funding. An agency/organization looks for funding that is a match to its mission and current services, and to the needs or problems to be addressed. The better the match between the funder's rationale for funding and the agency's mission and programs, the more likely the project will be funded and that it will be a successful project. In fact, it will be difficult for an agency to explain a request for funding that is outside its mission statement.

The first place a grant writer will look to begin to build an understanding of an agency is at its mission statement. The mission or purpose statement is developed by the board of directors of the agency (in voluntary agencies) or by other governing bodies (in public agencies), who create policy statements framing the agency's scope and its general approach to the broad problem. It answers the question "Why do we exist?"

Every agency's purpose is expressed in a mission or purpose statement which guides the agency through program development and community services planning. For example, Boys and Girls Clubs of America's mission is: To enable all young people, especially those who need us most, to reach their full potential as productive, caring, responsible citizens. The American Red Cross mission statement is: The American Red Cross prevents and alleviates human suffering in the face of emergencies by mobilizing the power of volunteers and the generosity of donors. Usually, the mission statement is fairly broad or global in nature, identifying the major issue the agency focuses on and a basic philosophy of how it is to address it. A mission statement may be so broad as to state: "To eliminate child abuse." Of course, we know that one agency cannot possibly accomplish this on its own; however, it tells everyone that this is what the agency is all about and the programs will be created to contribute to the elimination of child abuse. The agency might develop parenting programs, provide a public information campaign to prevent shaken baby syndrome, provide educational programs in the schools to help identify children in abusive situations, or hundreds of other programs within the context of its mission.

In addition to the mission statement, an agency may also develop a vision statement (and some add a values statement) to further describe their focus: for example, mission: to eliminate poverty; vision: every child receives a quality education and parents are gainfully employed; values: services delivered with respect and humility. To further elaborate on the mission statement and define action items, the Red Cross includes such things as communities are ready and prepared for disasters, or everyone in our country has access to blood (American Red Cross, 2016). (We suggest you conduct a search for mission and vision statements on the web. Look at both national and grassroots local agencies.)

It is easy to locate the financial statements for an agency as all agencies are required to file Form 990 with the IRS on a yearly basis. This form provides basic financial reporting as well as program highlights. When you view this document you can see the funding received by the agency and the amount spent in any given year. You can obtain this document through the organization called Guidestar.org, which provides a searchable database of thousands of agencies, making it easy for a potential funder or interested community member to obtain a copy of the 990 and learn more about the agency.

The working agency is staffed with the executive director or CEO who is the administrative manager overseeing the agency. She or he is hired by and reports to the board of directors who have fiscal oversight of the agency. The executive director hires and supervises staff, designs and implements

Figure 2.2   Simple Org Chart

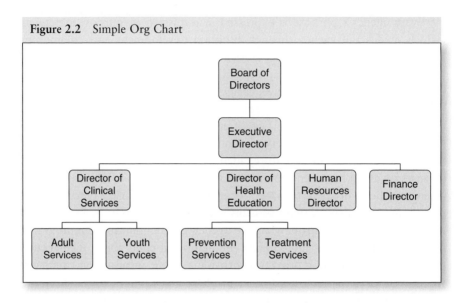

programs, develops funding, provides for the fiscal management of the agency, insures the agency is compliant with all regulations in their service area . . . in short, is responsible for the business. The nonprofit agency organization (org) chart looks like those of most businesses. There are program directors reporting to the executive director and service delivery staff reporting to the program directors, and so on. Figure 2.2 is an example of a simple org chart.

Organizational Capacity

Reviewing the agency's purpose, its past and current programs, and its future directions is a useful process. The following "Survey of the Organization" provides a format for examining the agency, for knowing what currently exists in the agency, and assessing agency strengths and weaknesses. The information you will obtain through this process will help you to screen requests for proposals to determine the proper fit with the organization as well as to develop a proposal which will move the agency forward with consistency and balance. We suggest you call an agency and ask if you can conduct an interview to learn more about what the agency does.

Survey of the Organization

1. Does the agency have yearly program reports and Forms 990?

2. What programs does the agency offer?

3. What is the agency service area (geographic area)?

4. What population(s) does the agency serve?

5. Is the agency adequately funded to meet its needs, or is it struggling?

6. Approximately how many grant applications does the agency prepare each year?

7. Does the agency offer client-centered services that are culturally appropriate?

8. Does the agency have a way for clients to provide input into the services they receive or want to receive?

9. Is the agency open and comfortable sharing information with you?

10. Does the agency keep records of services delivered?

11. Does the agency conduct research to determine the effectiveness of its services?

12. Does the agency have a good reputation in the community?

13. Has the agency ever been in a collaborative? What services have they delivered in a collaborative and what agencies did they collaborate with?

14. Request to see an agency organization chart (org chart).

Once you have completed this survey, you will have a better understanding of your agency, and you will be able to use this analysis to develop a new or expanded program that provides services in a realistic and manageable manner. Agencies are at various levels or stages within their focus areas and your proposal must demonstrate an ability to reach a new level of service. Agencies, like any business, can over-reach and develop too many products or too many activities that are not effective or sustainable. Too much diversity is a strain that can lead to system overload and program failure.

Consider the following example:

An agency has been providing educational programs to youth in schools and now wants to develop afterschool programs for teens. The agency realizes that it does not have community contacts with youth-serving providers and is therefore missing a major link needed to advertise and obtain participants for the new program. It does not have sufficient space to mount the program; therefore, the agency does not pursue the grant to provide educational programs. On the other hand, to address this shortcoming, the agency submits a proposal that provides for a process to create these linkages and develop this new network in order to be able to provide the full program in the future.

Working With a Collaborative

The term *collaborative* refers to cooperative partnerships and liaisons for service delivery. In the past, agencies provided a set of services to their identified client base, usually across large geographical areas. While these services were vital and necessary, they often were not sufficient to fully address the problem or meet the complex needs of the client. Furthermore, with agencies working in relative isolation from one another, it was difficult to know what other services were being provided and the costs of these services in total. Thus, the collaborative service model was born out of the community's need to

- provide coordinated and efficient services,
- address multiple and complex problems,
- contain costs, and
- improve access to services.

Beginning in the 1990s and continuing today, mergers became common in both the public and private sectors in an effort to bring escalating costs under control and to add "value" to products and services. Many nonprofit agencies either closed their doors during this difficult time or merged with other agencies. Agencies and funders began to look for new ways to deliver services more economically and efficiently, as well as with more account-ability for the results of services. It became common to hear funders use the term *outcomes-driven*, or state, "It is no longer good enough to do good in our communities. We have limited resources and we need to know what works. And, we must work together." Funders began looking at funding the nonprofit as an investment in the community, and, as in the for-profit-sector, the funder seeks a ROI—return on investment.

In the collaborative model, "communities" are redefined to better reflect actual interactive units of individuals, such as a religious commu-nity, a school community, or a particular neighborhood, rather than the broad geographical boundaries used in the past, that is, the XX County community or the Major City community. Service "hubs" located within the smaller community are created with an over-arching vision of "one-stop shopping" for program recipients. These hubs are sometimes referred to as *family resource centers*. Agencies bring their services to the family resource center and forge linkages with the community surrounding the center, as shown in Figure 2.3. This model is more convenient for the cli-ent in many ways; however, there are often some services that don't travel well, such as medical services requiring expensive equipment or labs.

As you can imagine, a collaborative can be structured in many different ways. Another common service design is to locate services within existing sites in the community such as a hospital or youth serving agency. Services from many different agencies can be offered at these sites. Figure 2.4 demonstrates a collaborative in which the clients will be asked to travel to various service sites to receive services.

Figure 2.3   Collaborative Model Using a Single Site

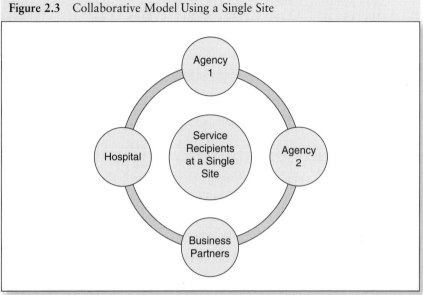

Figure 2.4   Collaborative Model Using Multiple Sites

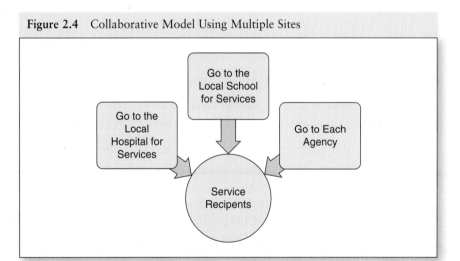

As is the case with service delivery strategies such as collaboration, there are advantages and challenges. The advantages of collaboration include the following:

1. Better knowledge of what services exist in a given area and what services are needed (service gaps)

2. More effective in meeting the interrelated and multiple needs of program recipients

3. More partnering between agencies resulting in new and creative service delivery plans—for example, the nutrition education classes of one agency delivered within the parenting education classes of another

4. Evaluation of the collaborative as a whole, providing the opportunity to see what difference multiple services make to a single program recipient

5. Increased access to program recipients

6. Increased ability to track the total amount of financial resources in a given geographic area

7. More flexible staffing through possible job sharing arrangements between the agencies—for example, it may be possible to hire one evaluator shared by all the partners, or one clinical supervisor, etc.

8. The development of personal relationships among providers to facilitate referrals and future program development

9. Increased participation of program recipient in service delivery planning

10. Increased access to local data (studies conducted by agencies or schools) and shared past proposals to help write the need statement for current proposals

The challenges of collaboration include the following:

1. Significant time spent in planning and at meetings

2. Some funding structures are not able to flexibly fund a collaborative

3. Potential problems between agencies regarding service planning and delivery structures

4. Sharing resources and taking shared responsibility for a mutual set of outcomes

5. Cost reimbursement issues if the lead agency is too small to manage the budget

A collaborative is a living partnership of people and bureaucracies. To be successful, the collaborative must have a shared vision, mutually developed goals, trust in the word of its leadership, a broad representation of collaborative members at the leadership level, and the ability to select and change leadership if necessary. Furthermore, the collaborative involves community members who receive services.

3

Finding and Applying
for Funding

Finding Funding

There are public and private funders offering grants. In 2002, in an effort to streamline access to and the submission of grants to the federal government, a portal called Grants.gov was established as a central storehouse for information on over 1,000 grant programs. Approximately $500 billion in annual awards are offered by 26 federal grant-making agencies in 21 categories, as shown in Table 3.1.

Most funding sources have missions or mandates to follow. In the case of governmental entities, the mandates are developed through legislative

Table 3.1   21 Categories of Federal Grant-Making

Agriculture	Arts	Business & Commerce	Community Development
Disaster Prevention & Relief	Education	Employment	Labor &Training
	Transportation		
Energy	Environmental Quality	Information & Statistics	Health
Housing	Humanities	Food & Nutrition	Law, Justice, & Legal Services
National Resources Recovery Act	Regional Development	Science & Technology	Social Services & Income Security

process and administered by the governmental agency; the resultant funding is allocated to address the identified need. Corporations and foundations may exist to meet certain needs, such as health foundations that were developed out of the transition from nonprofit status to for-profit structures. Other corporations may target particular issue areas that their board members or staff members want to address, such as afterschool services, day care services, job training and education, or domestic violence.

In addition to helping the community, most funders also look for positive returns from their giving. In some cases, this may be increased visibility and goodwill in a local community; in others, giving programs can lead to increased revenue. An example of this type of strategy can be seen in credit card use linked to charitable giving. If you use X card, the charity will receive a percent of your total purchase, thereby adding income to the charity. And, individuals who want to support the charity obtain the credit card, thereby adding income to the card issuer. Corporations are likely to view proposals favorably if they meet their own internal needs or promote the corporate image in the community. When writing these proposals, be aware of the WIFM rule—*What's in it for me?*—and seek to design a program having clear benefits to your target population as well as recognition for the funder.

The Federal Government

The federal government usually provides the most generous funding and the longest duration of any grants or contracts available, in fact, some government contracts have a three to five year term. Plus, unused funds in a government contract may be moved into the next year in a process known as *no-cost extension*. Federal funds are highly desirable and fiercely fought after. When a governmental agency has available funds they usually issue a *funding announcement* which provides the information needed to obtain a *request for proposals*, abbreviated as RFP. (We will use the term RFP in this book knowing that a funder may issue a request for applications (RFA), a request for quotes (RFQ), a request for bids (RFB), etc.) The RFP is the application packet containing the rationale for funding, full instructions, and required forms. Funding announcements (or sometimes called NOFA-notice of funding announcements) for the federal government can be found on Grants.gov or in publications such as the *Federal Register* at federalregister.gov or at the homepage sites for particular governmental agencies. If you know the federal division you want to apply to, you might go directly to its website and search.

For example, you might know that you want a grant from the U.S. Department of Health and Human Services (HHS), which distributes the largest amount of grant funding of any federal agency (http://www.hhs.gov/grants/grants/get-ready/index.html, 2015), letting a total of 32,000 grants in all. The web page will direct you to look at HHS grant opportunities listed under Grants.gov, to search at HHS GrantsForecast, and to subscribe to their *Faith-Based and Neighborhood Partnerships Grant Information Newsletter* via e-mail. (See Appendix B for Funding Resource Information.)

Federal government applications are generally prepared online through Grants.gov. which requires the agency be pre-registered on the site, as shown in Table 3.2. Registration is a project that can take four weeks or more depending on the agency's familiarity with the necessary components.

Table 3.2   Registering to Submit Federal Applications at Grants.gov

In order to use the federal government's grants management system the agency must do three things:

1. Register with Dun and Bradstreet to obtain a D-U-N-S: D-U-N-S stands for Data Universal Numbering system that identifies a business on a location-specific basis. It is the standard business identifier for federal electronic commerce. It can take 4 or more weeks to obtain this number.
2. Register at SAM or the System Award Management section of the federal government to designate an e-business point of contact (E-Biz POC) and authorized organization representatives (AORs)
3. Register with Grants.gov where the registration application can be completed by the end of the session when D-U-N-S and SAM numbers are available for use. It may take a week or two to complete this process.

Once this pre-registration is complete, the agency can apply for as many grants as they want without having to resubmit this information.

Once the registration is complete you can explore the online application. You will be able to cut and paste word document sections into the application. You can also upload agency documents like organization charts, a list of the board of directors, a yearly form 990, and other information requested by the funder. You can save your work on the site, edit when you need to, print and review, and, when you are ready, print your final copy and send it electronically.

Many RFPs are being issued as an online document. Whenever possible, save the entire document to your computer, give it a new working name, and fill it in. Save an extra copy as backup in case you have a problem with the first. Once the proposal is completed, save it again as its original name, print out a hard copy to review, and, if you are satisfied, send it back to the funder. Request an electronic receipt verification through your e-mail software if possible and/or directly from the funder once transmitted.

In other cases, online applications do not allow you to download and are challenging to navigate, so take some time to click on all the tabs and understand the structure before you begin. Most often, the budget pages of these documents are linked to other pages, so a numerical entry on page 15 for example, may change an entry on page 2. The best strategy we have found is read the form carefully, put in some test numbers (note the page you enter the numbers on) to see how formulas are set and how numbers move around in the proposal. Once you understand the logic of the budget section, delete all the test numbers you entered and start fresh in the proposal. If the document must be filled in online then perhaps you can print out the blank document first, prepare your answers, and then complete the document. Remember to check spelling and be sure to print the document before sending so that you have a hard copy of what was sent, date it, and file it.

The State and Local Government

State and local governments get their money in the form of state and local taxes paid by residents and businesses, from investment income, and from the federal government. When the state has successfully obtained federal funding for particular issues (the state often has to write a grant proposal to the federal government for the funding), the state may make the funding available to counties and cities. This kind of funding is called pass-through funding as the money comes from the federal government, to the state or local government, and, finally, to the nonprofit agencies. Some examples of pass-through funding include Community Development Block Grants (CDBG), Ryan White HIV/AIDS Program, and Medicaid funding. (Medicaid funding comes from the federal government to the state and consists of the amount the federal government will pay and the state will match. So, let's say, in California, the federal government pays 50 cents on the dollar with the county providing the other 50 cents of match to the state. In order to manage this, the county most often will require a grant application from the agencies who seek to provide Medicaid-reimbursed services in their jurisdiction, and they will develop a contract between the county and the successful applicant agency stating the services they are purchasing and the total amount available to the agency.)

Both state and city governments develop RFPs to enable competition for the funds; however, finding announcements of these available funds at the state, county, or city government website can be difficult. For example, you might want to start at your state or county website. For example, the state of California has a CA.gov/Grants website with some potential funding information but not all. Another resource that offers a more thorough listing of grants is GrantWatch.com (this is a subscription-based service) and, for example, libraries may have grant making resources such as the UC Berkeley library's list of grantors at www.lib.berkeley.edu/PUBL/grants.html.

In general, you need to work harder to find the state and local funding opportunities. You will need to go to the departments of interest at the state level—you can find a list of all of your state agencies at your state website. For example, let's say you want a grant for your high school mathematics and science students. You search the website of the California Department of Education and you find an announcement to develop a partnership between high schools and colleges and universities. You believe your school might qualify and you read the application. You think it looks like your school and project are a good fit. Then, you call the program contact person listed in the application and discuss the program you want to propose to see if it is a suitable match. You come off the phone knowing the funder's goals better and believe you can submit a competitive application.

You might also search by topical issue and location and see what is listed, such as, *HIV/AIDS Sacramento County*, or *block grant funding Oakland CA*. Each city involved in distributing community block grant funds will list the types of funding available and the application process on their city website. If you want to access county funding for specific services, it is best to call the county department offering those services and ask how you can learn about funding opportunities and to be placed on their notification list for new RFP's. For example, if you want to provide drug treatment services, contact the county department of alcohol and drugs. You might also want to contact other agencies in the areas that provide the types of services you want to fund and ask what grant opportunities they are aware of or can point you toward.

The Foundations and Corporations

Guidelines for the submission of foundation and corporate applications are typically found on the respective foundation or corporate homepages or through a variety of organizations such as the "FoundationCenterOnline" offered by subscription through the Foundation Center (New York), the United Way, or through searches online using keywords like, *corporate giving after-school programs* or *community giving AIDS*. Foundations and corporations are usually open to receive proposals early in the year until funds run out. Other foundations set fixed schedules to receive proposals, usually on a quarterly calendar.

Some foundations and corporations focus their giving on a local or regional level (e.g., Southern California), while others are national in scope. You will want to develop a list of the corporations and foundations funding your issues and serving your area, and visit each website to view their corporate giving or grants information. Looking at corporate websites will also help you assess the needs of the corporation in relation to their giving. For example, does the corporation appear to fund highly visible projects in which there is media attention giving a high public profile or does the company tend to give quietly to the community in which it is located? Does its giving tend toward opportunities to involve its employees through volunteerism? Does it have a specific list of possible interest areas? Look for a section on the corporate page to direct you to *Community Giving* or to the corporate foundation for more information about their giving. (If you are unable to find a link to the corporate giving program use the *Contact Us* link and make an email request for more information.)

While you are at the site, take the time to learn about the corporation or foundation and what it does. How is the business structured? How many facilities does it have? What type of product or service does it offer? Who are its customers? Having a familiarity with the company will help you to better target the proposal and help you to make an in-person presentation to the company if asked. You may also find it has a simple online application for small grants up to $5,000.

You may also find a fairly thorough listing of local corporations and foundations at your local United Way. Some agencies become a member of United Way to obtain funding for programs with United Way serving as a clearing house (it approves its members) and broker (it helps raise funds and supervise services for a percentage of the gross fundraising). An agency will go through an extensive vetting process to become a member agency and will also contribute to the fundraising efforts of the United Way organization.

Crowdsourced Funding

Much like a for-profit business would seek venture capital to develop a new product, the nonprofit sector is turning to the general public to support programs or even individuals in need through crowdfunding sites. Some of the crowd funding sites are Razoo, Kickstarter, Indiegogo, CauseVox, and Rockethub.com. Crowdfunding came into being as a way for individuals to gather support for specific needs in their personal lives or their communities. An individual may post a request asking for help to deal with an unexpected medical need or trauma and strangers will reply and donate money to the cause. You may be able to identify a particular aspect of your program that lends itself to crowdsourced funding—for example, providing scholarships for needy clients, purchasing computers or other technology for clients, or providing seed money for particular projects.

Search and Review

Yahoo!, Google, Bing . . . these are but a few of the search engines available on the Internet today. As you enter a few keywords (the main words in your topic), thousands of references containing those words pop up on the page. (These results may be different on each search engine used, so check several main search engines in your search.) Learning to search the Internet for relevant and reliable information requires a willingness to learn the language of search engines as well as the language of classification for the issue you seek information on. For example, you might enter *teen pregnancy* into a search engine only to find limited resources, while entering *adolescent pregnancy* yields an abundance of quality references. Experiment with a variety of keywords until you find the most salient information. Search engines usually have information on the page to help you use their search protocol most effectively and are worth reading.

The ability to access thousands of references in a single search will help you to find new treasures in the form of current data or new funding opportunities. We recommend that you create files on your "Favorites" menu to store the address of these websites for your future use—files named, for example, "Funders," "Demographic Data on X," and "Research Articles," as it is all too easy to suffer from information overload when conducting searches. For a more detailed description of search engines and using the Internet for research, we recommend an excellent book written by Susan Peterson: *The Grantwriter's Internet Companion* (Corwin Press, 2001).

As you compile information through the Internet, you will certainly find that some of it appears to be based in scientific fact and some is just opinion, or worse! This wealth of information requires a degree of discrimination on your part. Which information is reliable? Is this a reputable source or a homemade website taking this opportunity to promote an opinion? How can you tell the difference? To begin with, you will find that most of the information that is valid and useful to you will be found on the websites of well-known nonprofit organizations (.org), universities (.edu), and state and federal government offices (.gov).

The following questions will help guide you through the process of identifying a reputable, credible source.

1. Is the article published or not? If it is published, is it in a respected journal? Are there references listed in the article? Do you recognize the author's name or affiliation? There are many opinion articles on the Internet, so beware.

2. Does the site have product advertising and other "pop-up" ads leading you to believe that the information contained on the site is most likely to promote a particular product or viewpoint?

3. Do you recognize the name of the site as a reputable, trustworthy source for information such as the Red Cross, United Way, and the U.S. Department of Health and Human Services?

4. Are the data referenced on the site attributed to a source? For example, does it tell you where the data come from, such as a study by the Center for Disease Control and Prevention? If there is no reference as to where the data come from, be suspicious.

5. Does the website have the appearance of a quality site? Is it easy to navigate? Does it look professional? Is there information about the organization or company posted to the site?

Once you have located a few trustworthy sources of information, consult the references within each of those publications to find additional quality resources. You might also consult with a librarian who can help you find appropriate keywords for your search efforts and assist you in identifying authoritative sources. As you look at several reputable websites, you will begin to see that there is information that can be verified, there are references to other resources, there is information on the author(s) and the affiliations of the author(s), and information on the company or organization. You see little or no personal opinion, lobbying, or sales ads.

Table 3.3 provides some reputable websites to assist you in learning how to identify a quality site:

Table 3.3   A Sample of Reputable Websites

Centers for Disease Control and Prevention: www.cdc.gov
National Council on Aging's Benefits Check Up: www.benefitscheckup.org
National Institutes of Health: www.nih.gov
National Institute of Mental Health: www.nimh.nih.gov
Nutrition: www.nutrition.gov
Substance Abuse and Mental Health Services Administration: www.samhsa.gov
U.S. Department of Education: www.ed.gov
U.S. Department of Health and Human Services: www.hhs.gov

4

The Proposal Overview

The Components of a Proposal

A proposal is a comprehensive communication tool. It enables the applicant to express the need of the local community, to apply local solutions to problems, to state the value of (and the cost of) the proposed services, and the agency's unique ability to deliver said services. Much like the layers of a wedding cake, a proposal's sections need to fit and balance with each other. There are times where information is repeated from one section to another as questions may be similar—go ahead and repeat the information as the funder requests—this is often the case if the proposal is going to be "parted out" to reviewers who need some of the detail of a section but not all. The following listing provides a brief synopsis of the most usual components of a proposal while samples of each proposal section can be found in Appendix C.

1. **Letter of Intent:** Many funders will request a *letter of intent* or *letter of inquiry*, both abbreviated as LOI, in advance of submitting the proposal. This may be a request to assess interest in the funding opportunity so the

funder knows how many applications it will receive, in which case, a simple letter stating that you plan to apply will suffice. Or, it can request that you send a synopsis of the proposal you plan to submit with a brief summary of the project and the budget. In this case, the funder will determine if your proposal idea fits their guidelines and if they will allow you to apply. If this is the case, you will want to contact the funder's program officer (PO) in advance of preparing this letter to discuss the proposal ideas and to determine if the funder is interested. This will allow you to revise the plan to meet the funder's needs. After review, the funder will usually notify you in a letter inviting you to apply or rejecting your request to apply.

2. **Cover Letter:** A *cover letter* expresses the agency's interest in providing the specific services the funder has requested. The letter should indicate the agency's confidence in the attached proposal and the outlook of the agency toward a positive response from the funder. It may also include the title of the Request for Proposals (RFP), a number related to the RFP or project, the name(s) of the agency applying for funding, the name of the project for which funds are requested, a brief statement about what the project is and why it is important, and the amount of the request. The CEO or executive director of the agency and in some cases, the president of the board of directors or other appropriate official, usually signs it.

3. **Title Page and Abstract:** A *title page* is usually a form document provided by the funder in the application packet that provides the name of the applicant, contact information, and a brief summary of the proposed project known as an *abstract*. The abstract is often limited to 200 to 500 characters and is carefully crafted to present the project name, its general scope, and highlights of the project. It can be thought of as a mini press release on the project and should include enough detail about the project that a person reading the abstract understands what is being proposed.

4. **Need Statement (Also Called the *Problem Statement* or *Case Study*):** This is the heart of the proposal and it describes the community to be served and the problem or need being addressed by the proposal.

5. **Project Description:** This section describes the project or program submitted for funding under this proposal. The funder will specify how to present the project as to whether it will be established through the creation of goals and objectives or simply through a descriptive process. The funder may provide specific forms for this section called *Scope of Work* forms.

6. **Evaluation Plan:** The funder will want to know how the applicant will measure the success of the project. The agency submits an evaluation plan explaining what the project outcomes are projected to be and how

change will be measured. The evaluation plan will determine if the goals and objectives of the project have been met.

7. **Budget Request and Budget Justification:** The budget is developed to include detailed estimates of the expenditures of the project and it is usually presented in the format requested by the funder. An additional budget justification document is written to explain how the numbers were derived and how the funds will be used.

8. **Applicant Capability:** In this section, the applicant describes its experience in developing and providing services. This section often includes a history of the agency, a description of past project success, agency staffing, agency board of directors, awards the agency has received, a link to the agency website for client stories, and an organizational chart.

9. **Future Funding Plans:** Many funders are interested in seeing how the applicant can maintain the project into the future, perhaps by building in fee collection processes in the current plan or other avenues of income to support beyond this funding contract or grant.

10. **Letters of Support:** The funder is interested in seeing if other agencies or community members have an interest in seeing this project come to fruition. Letters reflecting community support for the proposed project from program recipients, community leaders, agencies, schools, or religious organizations are obtained and included in the application packet.

11. **Memoranda of Understanding:** If the proposal includes agreements between two or more agencies or organizations, most funders ask to see a written agreement from each of the partners or co-applicant agencies to be included in the grant application. The memoranda of understanding, also called the MOU or MOA (memoranda of agreement), is like a mini-contract stating what each party in the agreement will do and what they will be compensated and how.

12. **Appendix Materials:** This may include an audited financial statement, insurance documentation, the agency IRS determination letter, job descriptions, rosters, or any other documentation required by the funder. In some cases, the documentation requirement may extend to the partner agencies as well.

Proposal Submission and Scoring Process

A funding process consists of several steps until the final outcome is determined. Figure 4.1 illustrates a typical process.

In many cases a funder will hold a *bidder's conference* designed to enhance the understanding of the goals of the funder and offer specific details related

Figure 4.1   The Funding Process

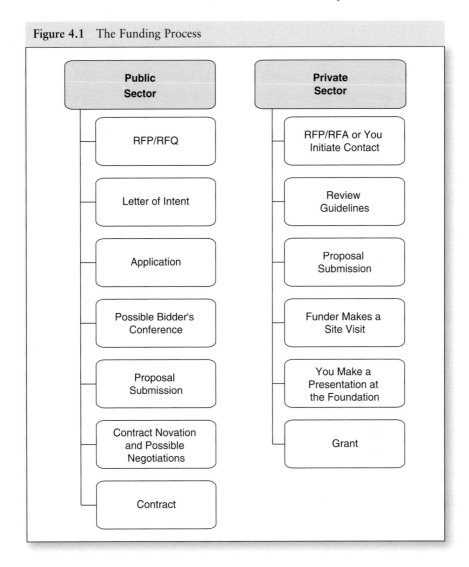

to proposal preparation. The bidder's conference provides the applicant with the opportunity to clarify the intent of the proposal and ask questions about the proposal in as fair a manner as possible. Prospective applicants receive a written transcript of the proceedings of the conferences held by the funder and of any questions they have answered over the phone. This provides a level playing field where all applicants have the same information. The conference also provides an opportunity to learn what other agencies are interested in submitting an application, leading to possible cooperative proposals and assessment of the competition. It is customary for the funder to provide attendees a roster of all attendees at the bidder's conference.

The proposal must be received by the potential funder by the deadline date. Submission deadlines will be included in the announcement and will determine the time frame for proposal preparation. Many governmental funders allow approximately four to six weeks between the funding announcement and the proposal due date. Funders are very serious about submission due dates. The funder will not accept a late application or any excuses. Any grant writer has stories of the horrors of being almost late or actually late with a proposal (which, in the case of a large application, represents hundreds of hours of prep time and potential lost revenue to the agency). One of the authors recalls missing a deadline to overnight mail the proposal to the funder and she purchased a plane ticket for a staff member to take a red-eye flight across the country to get it there by the 4 p.m. deadline. Every agency has these nightmarish stories to tell. *Plan ahead* is all we can say. Give yourself at least one extra day of lead time to get the finished proposal to its destination.

An additional step in the proposal process may be if the federal government requires that the applicant notify the state government about the funding request they are making. It may be a request to notify your state senator or other political figure. The application provides instructions and describes who to make contact with and when. (This is sometimes called a *single point of contact* request or SPOC.) It may suffice to send a copy of the proposal to the SPOC when the application is submitted to the federal office. We also recommend that you send a copy to your local legislators so they might advocate on your behalf.

Once the proposal is submitted and it has undergone a preliminary review, some funders will make site visits to the agency to meet the board, executive director, and staff members to insure that the agency is doing what it has indicated in the proposal. In some cases, the agency may be invited to make a presentation to the grantor's board of directors or staff.

Proposal Scoring

There is no single approach used for proposal review and scoring. Typically, government agencies create a panel of experts to review the proposal and they assign points for each section of the proposal. The review criteria and the weighting system to be used are sometimes listed in the agency's program announcements or application packets. In reviewing the proposal scoring criteria used by public and private funders supporting human service programs, our survey found they generally weighted the proposal sections as shown in Table 4.1.

It is a good idea to study the weighting system in advance and to spend the most time and effort in the most heavily rated sections. Reviewers may

Table 4.1   Proposal Scoring Weighting System

Proposal Section	Percentage
Project Description	25%
Need Statement	20%
Budget and Budget Justification	20%
Agency Capability Statement	15%
Evaluation Plan and Logic Model	15%
Appendix Materials	5%

meet together to discuss sections prior to assigning scores or may tally scores without meeting to determine successful applicants.

Foundations and corporations identify their proposal evaluation criteria in funding announcements, but are less likely to indicate the point values assigned to specific proposal sections. The community foundation and corporate funder is more likely to use staff to review the proposals while small family foundations may rely solely on family members. (We personally knew a family foundation member who opened the mail next to a 33-gallon trash can—interesting proposals went into a small stack and the remainder went directly into the trash. This observation led us to focus more energy on producing beautiful cover pages on quality paper with border art, catchy project titles, and succinct abstracts for our small foundation proposals!)

Funders are looking for projects that are realistic, that have measurable outcomes with a good chance for success, and that are ambitious. It is always attractive if the program reaches beyond known boundaries into unknown or untried arenas, which, if successful, will be a step into the future for the organization (and a nice success for the funder). Funders are especially concerned as to whether the agency can fulfill the goals for which the funding is provided.

In some cases, foundations may not issue formal RFPs instead, they will describe their area of interest and invite agencies to be considered for funding—these proposals are *solicited* by the funder who will not accept *unsolicited* proposals from just any interested candidate.

In addition to a well-written proposal, foundations give consideration to other factors in their decision-making process. We surveyed 164 foundations that ranked these as the top factors affecting whether an agency gets funded:

- Demonstrates a positive and measurable impact on those being served
- The proposal is from a collaborative or partnership

- Indicates a cost-effective operation
- Supports other organizations in the community
- Reflects cultural sensitivity and diversity
- Focuses on primary prevention of the problem
- Has a proven track record
- Establishes new, innovative programs
- Receives funding from other sources
- Has previous relationship with foundation
- Reputation of organization not too radical
- Has competent and professionally trained staff

In addition, the foundations revealed that two of the most common weaknesses in proposals are (1) not clearly identifying and substantiating a significant problem and (2) a lack of clarity as to how funds are to be expended for project activities.

Many times, one *well-placed* proposal has a greater possibility of being funded than one scattered indiscriminately to a variety of funders (also known as *shot-gunning*). Foundation and corporate development consultants are in contact with one another and are aware of a proposal that has been circulated in this manner and may look less favorably upon it.

A *notification of award* is usually mailed to the applicant and, in some cases, the successful applicant may be contacted by phone. In cases where the application is rejected and the proposal not funded, it is often possible to receive the scoring and reviewers comments. This is very helpful and strongly encouraged. On occasion, an agency may contest the outcome of the application process. Most governmental funders have a grievance process to follow if the applicant believes there is an error or oversight or wants to contest the determination. Details regarding this process will be found in the RFP packet.

In the best case, an award letter will arrive indicating that the application was successful and announcing the award amount. Sometimes this amount is less than applied for, and applicants will enter into negotiations with the funder. During these negotiations, the project description section and the budget section of the proposal will be modified to reflect the level of effort required under the funded amount. Or, a rejection letter will be received basically saying what a tough competition it was, and sorry your application fell short. One of the most important things a grant writer can do is learn to deal with rejection. Attempt to learn why the proposal was not successful and learn from the experience. A rejected proposal can easily become the foundation for a successful proposal if you can tolerate the rejection and grow from it.

5

Logistics and Basics of Writing the Proposal

The Nuts and Bolts of Writing a Proposal

We are preparing you to write a big state or federal proposal. These behemoths will disrupt your life for a brief period of time. In most cases, you will spend all your waking energy writing the proposal up to the deadline. You will want to activate your support people and prepare your home and work environment to best support you. It helps to have a work area that will be undisturbed so that you can leave materials out as you work. A portable file case can hold various materials and can be used to transport information if you are working at multiple sites.

If you are the main grant writer, you may also be working with an agency administrator and program staff from your agency and at least one or two others from participating agencies if you are writing for a collaborative. The main writer pulls it all together into one style, ensures that all of the materials are gathered up for inclusion into the grant, and makes certain that the grant application is in the format required by the funder. It is the responsibility of the main writer to read the Request for Proposals (RFP) carefully and in minute detail to comply with the technical aspects of the proposal preparation such as font size, margins, page limitations, page numbering, and so on.

Plan to have someone edit and proofread your proposal. In most cases, this will be someone who has worked with the grant writer in preparing the proposal so there is familiarity with the project. In addition to checking spelling and grammar, the editor should help to ensure that the main ideas in the proposal are clearly stated and that the proposal is internally consistent. All of the numerical totals in budgets should be double-checked by the editor as well. Finally, the editor should ensure that all attachments are included and the proposal is assembled accurately.

Although we have mentioned timelines that are imposed by the funder, the grant writer must also be aware of other processes the grant application must pass through before being ready for submission. It may need to be approved by the board of directors of the agency and partner agencies or the county board of supervisors. A board of supervisors, for example, meets monthly, so you may need to put the request in for signature before you have completed the entire proposal.

It is worth the time and energy it takes to ensure adequate supplies for the writing process in advance. Purchase extra printer, fax, and copier paper, copier toner, printer ink, stamps, large envelopes, file folders, pens, and large butterfly clips. Have overnight express mailing pre-addressed and stamped in preparation for a last-minute rush. Know where you can go to use a copier if yours breaks at the last minute, *and always back up your work*. (Remember to scan the thumb drive or other medium that is shared between different users for viruses every time it changes hands from one writer to another before reinstalling the proposal on your computer.) Finally, make sure you have a copy of the final proposal—not just on your computer, but a printed copy as well.

Writing for an Established Versus New Organization

There is a vast difference in approach if you are writing for an established organization or starting your own venture. An established organization has the clear competitive advantage, as it has a history in the community, has developed a successful funding track record, and has an established Board of Directors, programs, and staff. These are huge features to overcome in a newly formed nonprofit entity. If you are venturing out on your own, there are a number of features you will want to consider when writing your first proposal:

1. *Consider linking your program to an existing nonprofit with a similar mission.* Meet with the executive director and explore the possible fit. Develop a contractual agreement that spells out your relationship to the agency to protect your ideas and employability in the project once funded. Then, write the proposal and use the existing agency's track record to reach success!

2. *Involve persons in the project who have obtained and managed grants or contracts over their careers and use their experience and successes to build a credible foundation for your new entity.* This will help to demonstrate that you have the capacity to manage a grant project and the capability to implement the program you are proposing.

3. *Talk to the staff at the foundation you want to work with.* Make sure that your ideas are a good fit and that the foundation will consider a *first* proposal.

4. *Demonstrate support for your proposal.* You must have solid commitments from partner agencies as well as from the community you intend to serve. This is always an important feature but becomes even more important in this case as you must prove that the intended recipients of the services actually want and will use the services.

5. *Have an experienced grant writer review your work.* Consult as needed with staff in similar programs. Listen and learn from their experiences and build this knowledge base into the proposal. This will demonstrate to the funder that you realize that there are programs similar to yours and that you are willing to learn from them rather than reinvent the wheel.

6. *Establish a fair and reasonable budget.* Don't under-sell the project and set yourself up for failure and frustration or over-sell and make your bid unrealistic. You want to come in *on target* with the budget request.

7. *Realize that your passion to start something new is both a blessing and a curse.* The same enthusiasm that will endear you to some will cause others to shun you because, usually, passionate people don't listen. Be willing to see your idea morph into something similar but also different from the

original. Be willing to compromise to reach your goals. Remember, this will be your first program and you can continue to build the dream over time.

Writing for an Established Agency

If you are writing for an established agency, chances are good that you will be working in a small writing group or, at least, will need to obtain pieces of the proposal from others within the organization. The following ideas may be helpful to you in guiding the group grant writing process:

1. Establish the writing timeline early in the process and provide *due dates* to all involved. Make the date earlier than is actually needed to allow you time to bring it all together.

2. Establish a tracking calendar for all sections of the RFP to include letters of support, grant components, and budgetary items.

3. Ensure that the principal person who will manage the grant is involved in the program design and reviews the budget.

4. Serve as or assign a primary contact with the potential funder. This will ensure that there is no lost or misunderstood information between the funder and the agency. Keep a written log of the questions asked and the answers received, and share them with the grant-writing group.

5. Allow enough time in the process to provide a final draft to all involved. This step can help fine-tune the proposal and ensure that you have a great product.

6. Enlist the help of one trusted person to make necessary copies of the proposal. Ensure the proposal has been copied and collated correctly, bound, and mailed with some form of delivery confirmation. Keep a copy of the mailing receipt. An overnight mail delivery system is the recommended way to send the proposal—both for the tracking ability and for the receipts.

7. Establish a protocol for handing off the project once funded. Continue to track reports that are needed for the project for at least the first year to ensure that the project manager is giving timely feedback to the funder as requested. Provide the project manager with a listing of the needed reports, their time-lines, and the contact persons for the project. (This is above and beyond the expectations for most grant writers, but it is great for career advancement.)

Writing a Proposal for a Collaborative

When writing a proposal for a collaborative, the grant writer should be inti-mately involved in all phases of development to facilitate an understanding of the many aspects of the project and capture the richness of the effort. In some cases, the grant writer may be called upon to help develop the project and the proposal. One of the authors led a large collaborative for eight years and has developed a model for conceptualizing proposals in a large group. The following provides a brief summary of the three-part model that can be used by the grant writer to help the collaborative members organize their thoughts and services prior to writing.

Phase I: Determine the Need and Establish Goals

In this phase, program recipients and service providers define the needs. At a meeting all together or through several smaller meetings, the community and service providers create goals and place needs under the appropriate goal. For example, there may be a need for immunizations and dental care in the community as well as a concern about gang violence. Two goals could be developed: one goal addressing the health and mental health needs of children, and the second goal addressing community safety. The committee can make as many goals as they choose or use the goals provided by the funder under which local services can be organized. Once the goals are completed and needs fit underneath, the committee is asked to rank the community needs from most important to address now to less important to address now. (The definition and ranking of needs will help determine the asset allocation to follow.)

Phase II: Explore Potential Program Offerings and Benefits

In this phase, service providers propose what they want to do to address the needs, indicate which goal area it fits under, identify expected results and benefits, develop a budget, and provide a rationale for using this approach. In other words, are there any data or research to document the effectiveness their approach might have on reducing or eliminating the problem?

Phase III: Develop the Final Program Concept and the Budget

The program offerings are listed under goal areas. The amount of funding requested is placed alongside each program offering. The column is totaled, and, invariably, the budget needed exceeds the funder's allocation. Using the ranking system developed by the community and service providers, the whole group makes decisions about what stays as proposed, what might be adjusted, and what is eliminated from the proposal.

This process allows true collaboration to occur. In many instances, agencies are able to contribute some services *in-kind*, meaning that they will not receive money for these services; rather, they will pay for the services they are tying into the proposal. (By the way, some funders require a certain percentage of the proposal be *in-kind* contributions. We will address this issue further in the budget section of this book.) Furthermore, in this model, all agencies are part of the decision-making process, and the *lead* agency of the collaborative serves as a facilitator of the process.

Writing Style and Format

It is important for you to know who will be reading your proposal. Typically, readers of federal or state applications are professionals in the issue area of the request. They will know the jargon in the field and will expect you to use it freely and appropriately. (Merriam-Webster dictionary defines jargon as "the technical terminology or characteristic idiom of a special activity or group.") When you write a proposal to a foundation or corporate funder who receives requests in many different topical areas, the reader is most likely an educated generalist who knows a fair amount about many things. In this case, it will work against you if you use jargon. Contact the funder and ask who the reader(s) will be if it isn't clear.

Although not stated in the RFP, proposals that are written to governmental funding sources and some large foundations require a formal writing style. Avoid colloquial words such *cool, great, kids, guy, amusing, awesome,* and *wonderful,* and clichés such as "loads of" or "for many." In general, you will not use contractions, and you won't write, "I said," or "we think." Stay in the third-person. Don't use abbreviated words like *T.V.* or *photo*—spell them out. State your points confidently and offer firm support for your argument.

To demonstrate what we mean by the difference between highly formal and more "comfortable, friendly" writing style, here's a paragraph in which we say the same thing using each type of writing style:

Formal:　　　The sense of community in Nirvana is enhanced through the presence of farmer's markets, greenbelt areas, and ample parking. Each member of the board of supervisor's dedicates one day per week at the market place, and the mayor and city council members do likewise.

Less Formal:　Nirvana is a comfortable place to live with a weekly farmer's market, easy parking downtown, parks, and plenty of access to local government officials.

Just Wrong: It's lots of fun to live in Nirvana. There's just tons of things to do! You can go to the farmer's market and buy yummy fresh fruits and vegetables, or chat with the mayor and other elected officials.

A proposal prepared for foundations or corporations accepting applications in a wide range of topics may accommodate a more comfortable, friendly writing style fitting a more generalist reader who will be familiar with the topic but not immersed in it. Typically, the proposal is written in a more journalistic style, such as an article in *Time* or *Newsweek*.

You will need to find the appropriate citations in the literature to substantiate what you are saying. Unlike a research paper in which you use footnotes or endnotes to cite references, the references are usually incorporated into the body of the text. For example, one might write, "In 20xx, the birth rate for adolescents ages 15 to 17 in Orange County, California, was 38.5 per thousand (Orange County Health Care Agency)." Or, in another example, you may write, "According to a recent study conducted by the Children's Defense Fund (Annual Report, 20xx), latchkey children are at greater risk for stress related disorders." We hypothesize that this style of referencing developed as a practical response to space restrictions; that is, with a limited number of pages in which to present a case, you are likely to resist devoting one to references.

In all cases, the final proposal should be a clean document, free of spelling or grammatical errors. It should be visually pleasing with consistent section headers and typeface of a size and, if you had a choice, a font that is easy to read (think of the reader who has six of these to evaluate!). Charts, tables, graphs, and other illustrations can enhance the impact of the proposal and are now widely used. Avoid using shading or color graphs that do not copy well as a poor copy will detract from your proposal. (You may be able to insert shaded or color copies into each copy of the proposal in your packet if you think that the funder will not need to make additional copies to distribute to the readers.) Of course, if you uploaded the proposal to the agency portal, you need not worry about making copies for the funder, but do make hard copies of what you submitted for your own agency.

Using Audio/Visual Media

Some proposals lend themselves to the use of short video productions imbedded in the text or sent in digital format with the proposal to the funder. This type of visual project can have a significant impact on the funder. These videos are usually short, no more than about 2 minutes in length, and focused on the clients telling a compelling story about a topic you are addressing in the proposal. It is often possible to find students who need to produce videos for school projects to help you to produce a short piece.

Most of the materials that you create should be protected by copyright and we recommend that you check with agency administration before using or posting any images. This work will generally require copyrights and it will be protected. Conversely, you should be careful not to take (steal) the work of others and put it in your project without getting permission or consent from them. When this is difficult or impossible to do, there are photos available in the public domain that you can use without worrying about copyright issues. The photos that you find in your computer software programs are open-source photos and you can use them freely. You can also purchase the use of a photo from a stock photo store like iStockphoto.com, Shutterstock.com, or Getty Images. There are some free photos available from these sites as well. But, be careful about photos that you see on the websites of others and do not copy them without permission. Any time you take a photo or make a video clip you must have a release. We include a sample Photographic Release in Appendix D.

It is now a requirement that the agency have an attractive, effective, and up-to-date website that the funder can visit for more information. This site should have links to the board of directors, provide descriptions of the programs and key staff qualifications, have short videos on different aspects of service, feature the agency mission and values, link to annual reports and Form 990, and provide a clear way for persons to donate to the site. You should give your agency web address on all information pages and cite it in the Applicant Capability section of the proposal as well. (Remember to obtain permission for all photos used on the web page.)

It is a visual world and it helps if you can break up text using photos or graphics and charts. This is said with a caveat in mind—if you are restricted in terms of the amount of space you can use in the proposal, you may not have room to add a graphic or other visual. Make sure that any visual you use can be copied and still be effective and use colors or patterns in charts or graphs that can be differentiated in black and white print. Some basic types of useful charts include the following:

- Pie charts to show the different programs offered at the agency
- Column or bar charts to show the number of clients served by ethnicity or the population by ethnicity in the need statement section
- Organizational charts

6

Design the Program

Understand the Community Through Data

A good proposal begins with the collection of good data. You need to make a case that clearly shows that there is a substantial community need that should receive attention. It is often not obvious to people why programs are needed, and why your community should get money before other communities get funds. This chapter will take you through several steps toward understanding the problem and, ultimately, creating a program.

At this point, even though you may think you know what services you want to offer, it is important to keep an open mind about what the program might look like and let the data speak to you. The success of the proposal requires that you have a clear understanding of the nature of the problem you plan to address and that you have a sound approach for addressing it. The best way to reach this goal is to understand the factors that cause or contribute to the problem in the first place.

Have you ever gone without medical or dental care because you couldn't afford it? Have you seen homeless mentally ill persons pushing shopping carts up your city streets? These are examples of community needs because

41

they affect the quality of life of the population in a geographic area. Other examples include: the incidence of HIV infection, the number of babies born with birth defects, the number of persons who go to bed hungry, the incidence of high school drop outs, domestic violence or date rape, or, perhaps, the quality of air or water. In short, there is a problem in the community that requires attention, and this problem is expressed as a need. In defining the problem, Kettner, Moroney, and Martin (2008) state,

> A problem that is inadequately defined is not likely to be solved. Conversely, a problem that is well defined may be dealt with successfully assuming that adequate resources are made available and appropriate services are provided. Still, it must be understood that problem analysis is by nature more an art than a science. (p. 42)

They provide the following questions as a guide to problem analysis (pp. 45–49):

1. What is the nature of the situation or condition?

2. How are the terms being defined?

3. What are the characteristics of those experiencing the condition?

4. What is the scale and distribution of the condition?

5. What social values are being threatened by the existence of the condition?

6. How widely is the condition recognized?

7. Who defines the condition as a problem?

8. What is the etiology of the problem?

9. Are there ethnic and gender considerations?

Every community is unique. Think about the city you live in and those factors that define it—geographic, political, economic, and social components that make your city or town what it is. A quick visit to the website of your city will provide you with basic demographic information such as the number of persons living in the city, average age, average educational attainment, average income, and the number of children, working adults, and retired persons.

The following samples of data collection categories will provide you with a guide to the kind of data useful in both developing programmatic ideas and writing the need statement. You will want to obtain data on the following:

1. Incidence of the problem: whether the problem has increased, decreased, or remains the same

2. Clients' current physical, emotional, social, and/or economic status

3. Factors contributing to or causing the problem

4. Need in your target area to compare with other cities, counties, your state, and other states

5. Short- or long-term consequences of no intervention (including cost analysis if available)

6. Activities and outcomes of other organizations responding to the same or similar need, including any cost-benefit analysis

7. Demand for service: waiting lists, requests for service, lack of culturally appropriate services, and costs

8. Research studies on effective intervention strategies and evaluation results

Identify the interrelated components of a problem as illustrated below (see Figure 6.1)—there are usually many components causing a problem and these are often different in different areas of the country or among various populations and ethnic groups. For example, X Problem (e.g., homelessness) may be associated with Y factors (e.g., mental illness, unemployment, drug abuse). Social problems tend to be multi-dimensional and there is rarely a single factor that explains the phenomenon.

Figure 6.1 Problem Analysis

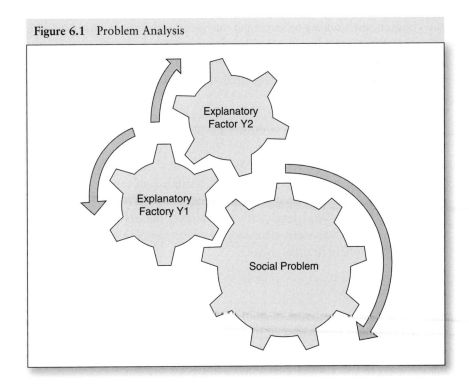

The following section identifies sources that you can use to find for the types of data just described.

Client/Community Needs Assessment

A needs assessment gathers information about the client's/community's perception of the problem and needs. This type of assessment is usually conducted through interviews with program recipients, through focus groups, or with questionnaires. Many agencies have conducted needs assessments and may be able to share the results with you, such as a local health care council or the United Way. These documents are invaluable to making a case for your project. If you conduct an assessment on your own, it is important to involve members of various ethnic groups (stakeholders) who experience the problem and who will benefit from the proposed program as well as individuals who serve this population. You may find that there are different perspectives on the problem and different solutions.

City, County, and State Demographic Data

Most county governments and universities compile information about the residents in geographic areas based on U.S. Census data conducted every 10 years. These demographic data provide such things as the number of adults and children, the number of single-parent households, the income level, the educational level, and housing density. Some university-based research centers have *geo-mapping* (geographic information systems) capabilities that allow a user to define a geographic area and extract demographic data and other indicators for that region.

Specific problems or issues are often tracked by county government and by state departments working in those issue areas. Teen pregnancy rates, for example, may be found at the County Health Care Agency or child abuse rates at the County Department of Social Services. Community-based organizations will frequently have data already compiled on certain community problems. The most organized of these agencies will have the incidence of the problem at the local level (city or county), the state level, and the national level. It is frequently necessary to determine how your geographic area's needs compare to other areas.

Journal Articles

There is a rich storehouse of information in scientific journals. You will find research into the causes of problems as well as research on effective solutions to the problems. From meta-analysis of the effectiveness of various program designs to studies on a single program's effectiveness, you will be happy to see that there is a wealth of information on the effectiveness of different program approaches in various populations. When you draw upon this information and select a known and effective intervention, you are said to be using "best practices" or an "evidence-based" model. In addition, the bibliographies in the articles in academic journals can help a newcomer to a particular field find other important work quickly.

Local Newspapers

Articles in local newspapers can be another resource to help the grant writer develop a sense of the community perception of the problem and of local resources. (However, the grant writer must be cautioned not to depend solely on newspaper reports, as their articles are only as accurate as their informants.) A local newspaper can assist in identifying local leaders and current events in communities.

Formulating Program Ideas

The previous section of this chapter helped you to think about developing a program with those to be served foremost in your mind. It also challenged you to look beyond your own ideas about what might be a good program idea and review the scientific and professional practice literature. You have also been advised to consider the capacity of the agency or organization to successfully launch the project and to think of ways in which all or parts of the initiative can be sustained post-funding.

You now need to refine your thinking and hone your ideas in order to formulate the specific direction you are heading with the proposed program. Similar to a funnel, you start with a number of ideas and directions that could address the need/problem (see Figure 6.2). You consider these in light of current resources, opportunities, agency capacity, as well as constraints, along with any parameters that the funder may have. Ultimately, you develop a program that you believe will achieve the desired results and address the need/problem.

As you read through the next nine steps, you will gain a good sense of the different components of the proposal. The following process will introduce you to new components such as goals, objectives, and implementation activities to name a few. We are going to take you through our nine steps to develop the beginning of a proposal and continue to expound on these steps in the remaining chapters.

Step 1: Understand the need/problem. Answer the questions: What is the problem? Why is this a problem? Who is experiencing the problem? Is it

Figure 6.2   Formulating the Proposal Idea

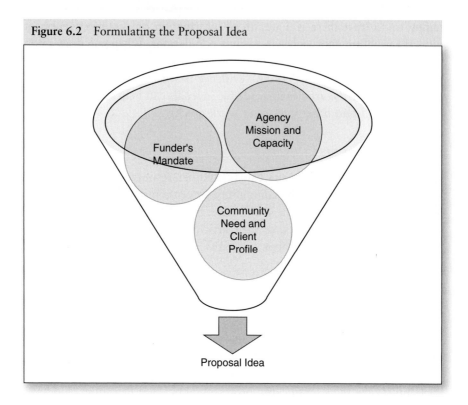

recognized as a problem/need, by whom, and how widespread is it? Are there social/political implications? What factors contribute to the need/problem?

Step 2: Brainstorm solutions. Think creatively and freely about what might be done to address this problem. Dream of what might be possible and effective in creating change and positive results. Examine the scientific and professional practice literature to mine successful program ideas and use "best practices" when developing your plan. Consider the strengths and resources within your target population, the agency, and the community that can be coalesced to achieve positive results. Make a list of all of the ideas you and your team generate. Develop two or three program goals that are statements of the ultimate mission or purpose of the program you are proposing. (In some state or federal Request for Proposals, the goals are given.) Goals are often lofty and future-oriented statements such as (1) to eliminate birth defects in Grant County; (2) to prevent child abuse; (3) to make our oceans and streams pollution free; (4) to eliminate tobacco use; (5) to improve health outcomes in Grant County. The idea is to use a goal statement as a hoped-for outcome for a project. Goal statements are also used to identify major sections of the program, and it is useful to have several goals if the program is serving distinct populations or offering distinct types of service.

Step 3: Select solutions and describe results. Identify the best program ideas from your list that will achieve your goals and write these in the form of an objective. Objectives identify the target to receive the service and the *expected* results. They provide the "promise" of what will be achieved over the course of the funding period. Objectives are specific, achievable, measurable statements about what is going to be accomplished within a certain time frame, and usually focused to address the various causes of the problem. It is also useful to think of objectives as the steps that you will take to reach the goal. For example: The goal of a program may be "to eliminate child abuse." Objective 1 may state that "Fifty (50) high-risk families will improve family functioning by 25% by June 30, 2019," or "Twenty (20) abusive parents will increase their coping skills by 50% by October 30, 2019." Each program goal will have at least three to four objectives. (More in the evaluation chapter.)

Step 4: Think about barriers. Insure that the target population can participate as fully as possible. For example, a brick-and-mortar clinical services model to provide health care services may miss seeing clients who have no transportation to the clinic. Or another clinic may not be able to attract Spanish-speaking clients as there is no Spanish-speaking staff to greet them. The reasons why a client does not access service are known as *barriers* to service.

Barriers may exist as a result of a client's orientation to services wherein he or she may lack the knowledge, desire, or skills necessary to seek treatment or prevent a problem. An example of this type of barrier exists in drug treatment services when the client denies that he or she has a problem. The client may also hold attitudes or beliefs that are not compatible with the seeking of certain types of services. For example, an individual who uses traditional cultural healers may not value the services offered by Western doctors. Many times, however, barriers are created by the service providers themselves or through the program design and are usually assessed in five domains:

1. *Availability*: Are services provided in the community, or is the cost prohibitive? Are the hours of operation convenient for the client?

2. *Accessibility*: Can the client get to the site? Does it take special physical needs into consideration such as handicap access? Is there transportation to and from the site? Are there eligibility criteria that may influence accessibility? To what

extent are multiple services provided at a convenient single location?

3. *Acceptability*: Are the services in the client's language and sensitive to cultural issues? Is the staff perceived as friendly, professional, competent, and helpful? Is the decor and design of the service setting inviting to and respectful of the client?

4. *Appropriateness*: Is this the right service for the client? Will this service address the problem as the agency expects?

5. *Adequacy*: Is the service sufficient in amount and approach to meet the individual or community's needs? Are services as comprehensive as possible?

Step 5: Think about sustainability and the life cycle of this project: A funder may ask, "Do you plan to continue this project in the future? If so, how do you plan to support or fund it?" In the majority of cases, the answer to the first question will be "Yes," followed by a brief description of how the program may be developed in the future. The answer to the second question may be more problematic for the grant writer. Human nature being what it is, we are more likely to have fixed our minds on obtaining the initial funding for the project rather than concerning ourselves with the funding of the project beyond the current request.

If you view the question from the funder's perspective, you will realize the wisdom of this inquiry about future funding. It is nice to support projects that will do wonderful things over the course of the funding, but rather frustrating to find that they simply cease when your funds are no longer available. From a funder's perspective, it is reasonable to look for projects that have the potential to continue the work into the future.

You may know of other funding sources who will want to fund the project in the future. Or, you may find ways to continue the project without funding, as in ways to "institutionalize" your project, meaning, to imbed it into existing service delivery systems such as schools, hospitals, churches, or other agency services. Or, you may explore whether the project has the ability to receive income from the project itself, building a way to support the project later on. Ask the following questions:

- Can the program charge a fee-for-service or receive a donation from the clients?
- Is it possible to market products or materials developed under the project to other agencies or businesses?
- Can the agency turn the program into a service that the community at-large will pay to receive?

Step 6: Determine tasks to accomplish solutions. These are known as *implementation activities*. There are two kinds: activities that are preparatory to starting a program, and the activities that describe the deliverable or promise of each objective. As the above objective says: Fifty (50) high-risk families will improve family functioning by 25% by June 30, 2019, and an implementation activity will describe the services that the families will receive to reach this objective: for example, a 12-week educational program on family communication skills.

Preparatory activities prior to the start of services include ideas such as the staff needs to be recruited and hired, participants need to be located and recruited for service, facilities need to be identified and prepared, and program materials need to be created or ordered. Once the program starts, activities include the actual services as scheduled and delivered, tracking and documentation of client participation, and program evaluation is conducted on schedule and in the prescribed manner (More on this in the evaluation chapter.)

Step 7: Estimate resources needed. What are the resources needed in both human and monetary terms? What do you estimate the proposed program components will cost? Will the total available funds be sufficient to cover the cost of the project? Although we encourage free thinking to generate proposal ideas, it is time to ground in reality. Take some time now to briefly assess the cost of what is being proposed (more detail on this is in the budget chapter). Take a quick look at the big ticket items: staffing, rent, and indirect costs. Estimate the cost. Revise the program accordingly.

For example: You are writing a proposal for a $20,000 foundation grant. You want to offer an afterschool program from 3 p.m. to 5 p.m., 5 days a week for 12 weeks for 25 youth. You want to contract a credentialed teacher, a physical education instructor, and a counselor to be present the entire time. The rate for the teacher is $100/hour times 10 hours for $1,000/week or $12,000 per summer. The PE instructor is $50/hour times 10 hours for $500/week or $6,000, and the counselor is $80/hour times 10 hours for $800/week or $9,600. You can quickly see that the design is not supportable.

You might want to solicit in-kind donations—which is when products or services are donated to the agency—to reduce the amount of funding requested. For example, if the project plans to publish a newsletter, you can find a local printer who will provide a donation of printing to the agency. Or, you might receive a donation in the form of books, office supplies, or furniture. People may donate their time and skills to the program in-kind, which can be counted as funds to offset the grantors funds. (See the budget chapter for more on this topic.)

Step 8: Make necessary adjustments to solutions and benefits. The hard reality is that most of the time we think of programs that cost more than the available funding, or we find an insurmountable barrier or other problem in implementation. We have to make some adjustments in the project.

Try not to let yourself be discouraged by this—the ideas may be used in future programs and services.

Step 9: Identify measurement of outcomes. How will we measure success? What evidence is needed to determine whether we have been successful? We have said that we will improve family functioning, increase knowledge, and build skills. We will determine what we will use to measure success such as pre- and post-tests, standardized tests, or observation, for example. (We will address this in greater detail in the evaluation chapter.)

Figure 6.3 summarizes the process of developing a program as you identify the problem, develop approaches or services, conceptualize measureable outcomes, reassess the impact on the problem, and either keep or modify the plan.

Once you have completed these steps you will have developed a very substantial program. The authors have always felt that we could improve upon the program designs we have created, no matter how many times we returned to it. There is always something that can be improved upon. However, there comes a time when you will want to let it go and move on. Once a program is funded and you have the opportunity to "see it in action," you will bring new ideas and improvements to future iterations of the project.

Figure 6.3   Addressing the Problem

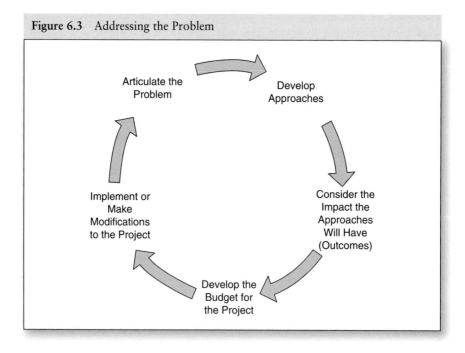

7

Program Objectives and Evaluation

Evaluation

You can't go too far in thinking about a program without considering what changes the program may bring about in the client, the community, and even the provider. (Note: When submitting a proposal you will be expected to prepare the evaluation plan following your description of the proposed project. By placing this chapter here we are trying to provide you with the opportunity to be aware of the impact the evaluation may have on the program design. We want you to understand that the evaluation plan is tied to the project's goals and objectives.) When you design an evaluation plan, you are seeking to determine whether the stated project components or objectives were achieved. The objectives represent the "promise" and the evaluation provides evidence that the promise was fulfilled. In this chapter, we will focus on *process* and *outcome* evaluation. (If you need additional help seeing how the project ties to evaluation, you may want to read the "Program Design and Evaluation Case Study" in Appendix D.)

A process evaluation provides an assessment of the procedures used in conducting the program, hence the term "process" rather than "outcome." A primary goal of this type of evaluation is to gather feedback information during the operation of the program to determine how the service was delivered or how the client was recruited. For example, let's say you want to know which outreach efforts result in getting the most people into programs: phone calls, flyers, directory listings, websites, newspaper articles, or other forms of outreach. Conducting this type of research may include:

- one-on-one interview of participants of the program,
- detailed tracking of staff efforts in outreach efforts,
- assessment of administrative and programmatic functions and activities, and
- detailed accounting of how each participant heard of the program.

The results can be used to improve the implementation of a subsequent program with a similar focus. Process evaluation provides an understanding of how you achieved the results; that is, it describes what happened, how the activities were accomplished, and at what level of effort. When you conduct a process evaluation, the objective is written to indicate a process evaluation is needed. So simply stated, there are process objectives and process evaluations.

Process evaluations can be written, for example, on the following:

Training or Education Programs

1. What is content of the training? What are the unique features of the training?

2. How is the training conducted? What procedures, techniques, materials and products are used? What is the background of the trainer(s)? What costs are associated with the training?

3. What is the background of individuals trained, and which training techniques are most effective with which groups?

4. What are staff's perceptions of the quality of the training? How can it be improved? What level of effort is required to accomplish each facet of the training?

Products/Materials Development

1. What and how are the products/materials developed and tested?

2. How are the products/materials disseminated?

3. How are the products used, including how often, by whom, by how many?

4. What are user and staff perceptions about the products/materials?

5. What is the cost savings associated with the products/materials?

Improving Operations or Procedures

1. What is the nature of the improved operations or procedures? How do they contrast with the previous ones?

2. What is the implementation process for the new procedures or operations?

3. How do the new procedures or operations affect service? Contrast cost savings and level of effort between old and new.

Although process evaluation can be very valuable in understanding how things work and how things can be improved, the reality is that they are used infrequently due to cost constraints.

The most common type of program evaluation is known as an *outcome evaluation* or a *results-based evaluation*. This type of evaluation is used to determine how well the program met and achieved its objectives. It focuses on the "what" or "how much" was achieved. What changes occurred in the program participants or community conditions as a result of impact of the objective? This type of evaluation is sometimes referred to as the "so what" of the program; that is, *so what* happened, *so what* was accomplished, and *so what* difference did it make?

Figure 7.1 illustrates the conceptual framework for developing a results-based, outcome evaluation plan. You can see that the project will seek to measure the promise contained in the objective to improve prenatal nutrition by conducting pre- and post-self-reports of the participants. In this case, the participants will be asked to provide information about what they ate both at the start and at the end of the program. (Note that the *implementation plan* itself is stated within this evaluation framework but that the evaluation itself is tied to the objective. This is here to show the complete objective.) The program will be able to determine a change in the nutrition of participants with this evaluation plan.

Four Steps to Preparing the Objectives and Evaluation Plan

Step 1: State the Expected Outcomes or Results

We look at the program goal, which in this case is to eliminate obesity in college-age youth, and then we itemize the program components you

Figure 7.1   Results-Based Evaluation Framework

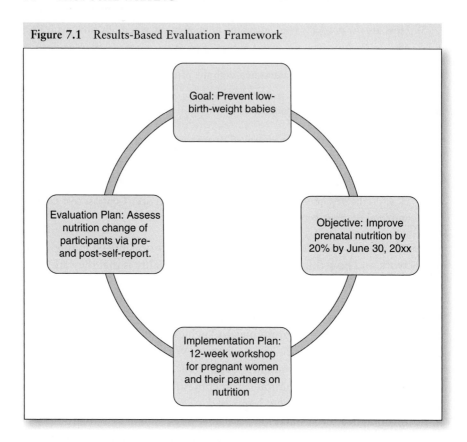

plan to address that contribute to causing obesity in college-age youth. The components we want to work with are (1) poor nutrition, (2) lack of exercise, (3) depression, (4) lack of access to healthy foods.

First Objective: Improve the nutritional intake of 200 college-age students by 25% by June 30, 20xx.

- It provides the number and type of participants. Check.
- It specifies what is expected to happen with the students. Check.
- It provides a timeline of the service. Check.

Second Objective: 80 self-identified, sedentary college-age students will increase their activity by 25% by June 30, 20xx.

- Meets the criteria above? Check.

Third Objective: 20 students with depression will increase their knowledge about the causes and cures for depression by 20% by June 29, 20xx.

- Meets the measurable criteria above? Check.

Sometimes so-called proxy outcomes are developed. For example, you may wish to improve birth outcomes by decreasing the incidence of low birth-weight babies. However, this may be very difficult to measure. At the same time, research has shown that there is a direct link between women receiving early prenatal care and improved birth outcomes. Therefore, one can use getting women into early prenatal care as a "proxy" measure for the desired outcome of improved birth weight.

In many cases, the program will not only achieve short- and long-term outcomes for the participants, but may also have a long-term impact on the community or society at large. For example, the cumulative effect of women participating in this prenatal program may also lead to an overall improvement in the county's health care indicators. Such a long-term evaluation can be a costly evaluation design, and so it is rarely completed. We use short-term measures to view change in the steps toward the goal.

The beginning grant writer is apt to confuse an objective with an implementation activity. A common error is to write the actual program or service that is going to be offered without indicating its benefits. Such an error would result in the following example of a *poor* objective:

> One thousand youths between the ages of 12 and 16 will participate in a six-week education program on violence prevention by June 30, 20xx.

In this example, the "six-week education program" is an implementation activity and does not describe what the impact will be on the participants regarding violence prevention. The following questions may help the writer to reach the outcome level of the objective: Why are youths receiving a six-week program? To increase their knowledge or improve their skills? To change behavior? A revised, well-stated objective would look like this:

> One thousand youths between the ages of 12 and 16 will increase their knowledge by 40% in conflict resolution and anger management by June 30, 20xx.

Depending on the length of the program or service and the nature of the intervention, changes may occur at different rates. It may be easier to increase one's *knowledge* about a subject (short-term outcome), but take longer to *change behavior* (intermediate or long-term outcome).

Examples include the following:

- Increase knowledge about healthy foods (short term)
- Reduce body mass index (intermediate or long term)

As you write your objectives, make sure you are stating the expected *outcome* or changes in the program recipients, and not just identifying the approach being used. In summary, the following example shows how a single goal can lead to several process and outcome objectives:

Sample Goal 1: To prevent drug use among young people by promoting their academic success and emotional well-being.

Process Objectives:

Sample Objective 1:

To form a coalition of ten youth-serving agencies in order to develop a comprehensive plan for providing after school activities at two junior high schools by June 30, 20xx.

Outcome Objectives:

Sample Objective 1:

One hundred at-risk junior high school students will increase their knowledge by 60% about the dangers of drug and alcohol use by June 30, 20xx.

Sample Objective 2:

One hundred junior high school students who are academically at-risk will show a 30% improvement in their reading and math scores by June 30, 20xx.

Sample Objective 3:

One hundred parents will increase their knowledge by 40% in effective communication techniques for teaching their children about decision-making, goal setting, and the dangers of drugs by June 30, 20xx.

To recap:

- The *goal statement* provides a general aim and direction for the project, but lacks in specificity as to what will be achieved.
- *Process objectives* identify the approach to be used but do *not* state what impact it will have on the participants. (It is not necessary for every proposal to have both process and outcome objectives. Process objectives are written when a funder has indicated that the desired outcome is to develop a new approach or test a method of service delivery.)

- *Outcome objectives* specify "who" and "how many" are to achieve "what results" by "when."

Common errors in writing objectives include (1) putting more than one measurable outcome in the objective and (2) saying much more than is needed in the objective. Keep the objectives simple and clear. While you want to "stretch" as far as possible with a vision for improved conditions or circumstances, objectives should be realistic and not promise more than can be delivered within the time period stated. Remember also that objectives are directly tied to the contractual relationship between the agency and the funder, and, as such, the agency may be held accountable if the objective is not met.

Step 2: Determine the Type of Evidence Needed

Now let's look at the kinds of things we can measure so we can develop a measurable outcome for each component. We want to know if the outcome happened as projected in the objective. To determine this, we need to know how to measure change. The usual change indicators are known as KABS:

- Knowledge—What does the individual know about this issue, and can increasing their knowledge impact the way the person relates to the issue? Can knowledge prevent problems?
- Attitudes—How does a person feel in relation to the problem? Does their belief set contribute to their participation in the problem? Is their belief set harmful to themselves? Can it be changed?
- Behavior—How does the person act? Do they say one thing but do another? Impacting behavior is considered to be high-level change as people can say they will, but until they incorporate that change into behavior, it is all talk.
- Skills—Does the person want to change but just lacks the skill set to accomplish this? For example, they are emotionally ready to work but don't have a driver's license, or they can't read. Skill development would lead to improved outcomes for this client.

The easiest type of indicator measure is knowledge change because you can give a pretest before the intervention to determine the amount of knowledge a person currently has and then give a post-test to determine the amount of knowledge the person has at the end of the service and calculate the difference. (Here is a simple formula to determine percentage of change: *(1) subtract the old value from the new value, (2) divide that number by the old value, and (3) multiply by 100 to convert that rate to a percentage. Example: A student score on the pretest was 82 points and 92 points on the post-test. 92–82 = 10. 10/82 = 0.1219 x 100 = 12.19% or simply 12%.)*

It is often more difficult to determine change when it comes to behavior. In most cases, the evaluation plan will take a "self-report" from the participant to determine current levels, and then another self-report at the end of the intervention or treatment to determine change. Another way to measure behavioral change is to observe the client in the new behaviors.

This leads us to another issue: sample size. The usual rule of thumb is to sample 10% of the group up to a group size of 1,000. Or, another way to determine sample size is to use the Krejcie and Morgan Sample Size Table (in Appendix D) which provides you with greater accuracy. You can select your method based on what degree of precision you need in your sampling. (There are websites to assist in evaluation; one good site made by young professionals is at www.kenpro.org.)

As you develop the evaluation design, be aware of the tendency to overpromise outcomes and to use very large sample sizes. People will normally drop out of programs, and some people will not change as much as others. You want to strike a balance between providing the most robust evaluation you can and overpromising.

As you can see, determining the appropriate measures that represent the expected results takes time and an understanding of the changes your approach will yield. In recent years, there have been compilations of indicators typically used in human services programming and much of the program evaluation data can now be found on funder's websites. For example, you can visit Centers for Disease Control and Prevention and review studies that have been conducted on obesity and see the indicators and measures they used. The following list provides examples of common indicators:

Healthy Births

- Increased knowledge about prenatal care
- Lower rates of low-birth-weight babies
- Higher rates of prenatal care in the first trimester

Substance Abuse

- Increased knowledge about the dangers of alcohol and drug use
- Duration of abstinence
- Number of relapse events

Parent Functioning

- Improved scores on parenting skills
- Increased time spent reading to children
- Reduction in parental stress and family violence

Education

- Dropout rates by district
- Percentage of third graders who read
- Standardized test results and report cards

Mental Health

- Depression and anxiety indicators
- Stress measures
- Overall functioning and quality of life indicators

Step 3: Determine the Data Collection Plan

The next step is to identify the evidence that represents the achievement of the outcome objectives. There are usually two parts to this: first, did the number of participants stated in the objective actually participate? How can a project count this? Did the activity actually take place? The ways in which this data can be collected include the following:

- Participant sign-up and sign-in sheets (which are most useful if you have to prove that an individual actually participated in a class or activity)
- Agenda and minutes of meetings
- Visitor logs
- Written requests for products or services
- Participant interviews
- Movies or photos of the event and participants
- Staff schedules, calendars, or phone logs
- Newspaper articles about the activity
- Direct counts

The second part of the data collection plan is to measure the change in the client. The ways in which these data can be collected include the following:

- Pre- and post-testing of client knowledge
- Assessment, or survey of attitudes, values, and beliefs
- Observation
- Individual interview
- Focus groups (a form of interviewing in a group)

(There are a variety of publications of tests that can help you measure family functioning, self-esteem, coping skills, cognitive functioning, anxiety, depression, aggression, anger, eating, activity, etc. Many of these can be administered by anyone [some have restricted use to licensed professionals].

You can start a search at Mental Measurements Yearbook, Tests in Print, or Standardized Tests and Measure to name a few.)

Step 4: Identify Data Analysis and Reporting Procedures

Now that we know what we want to measure as an outcome, we need a data collection plan. Let's consider the following:

1. Identify the person(s) in the project who will be responsible for developing or selecting the data collection tools.

2. Consider when the data will be collected—at entry, at first service, at midpoint, at the end, or in follow-up?

3. Will the evaluation design require there to be any comparison or control group(s)? These would be comparable people who don't receive the service.

4. Are the tools likely to meet the needs of the cultures involved or will there be a need to find specific cultural appropriate measures?

5. Will the evaluation require human subject protections including assuring voluntary participation in the evaluation, proper treatment protocols, and protection of client confidentiality, etc.? Who in the project is responsible to insure this is completed?

6. Sampling plans, including type of sample, and size (if applicable, see Sample Size table in Appendix D).

The federal government has developed a data collection protocol known as GPRA (pronounced gip-rah). This is short for the Government Performance and Results Act law enacted in 1993 to improve government accountability. Basically, the law requires that all contractors with the federal government meet the criteria established by the law and comply with data collection protocols submitted to the Office of Budget Management each year. The GPRA requirements will be stated in the proposal application packet. (The GPRA mandate is in Appendix D.)

Evaluation data are usually presented to the funder on either a quarterly or semiannual basis and at the project's end. Project data should be presented in a graphically rich format—using charts and graphs to illustrate the outcomes.

A Logic Model

The program components you have developed can now be incorporated into a *logic model* which, according to Knowlton and Phillips (2009), is a visual method of presenting an idea. They offer a way to describe and share an understanding of relationships among elements necessary to operate a program or change effort. Logic models describe a bounded project or initiative: both what is planned (the doing) and what results are expected (the getting). They provide a clear roadmap to a specified end. (p. 5)

Table 7.1 presents a logic model format with expected content. (Various funders may have different format expectations.)

Table 7.1   Sample Logic Model

Inputs-Resources	Process-Activities	Outputs-Measurements	Outcomes-Changes/Benefits (Short, Inter-mediate, or Long Term)	Impact on the Community (Long Term)
Human Resources • Staff • Volunteers • Consultants • Clients Material Resources • Facility • Travel • Communi-cations • Project Materials • Technology	• Education • Training • Counseling • Health care activities • Evaluation and assessment	• Number of persons who attend • Number of persons who complete • Number of hours associ-ated with services and activities • Client logs or sign-in sheets • Pre- and post-tests, physical exams, or other obser-vational measures • Materials produced • Participant feedback about services	• Increased number of healthy meals eaten each week • Reduced body mass index • Lowered blood pressure • Elevated mood and reduced depression	Improved community health indicators: • Reduced diabetes • Reduced heart disease • Reduced sick time away from work

Writing the Evaluation Section

Program evaluation may be presented in a narrative form, an outline, or on a funder-developed form (we will use a scope of work form in the next section). If no specific instructions have been given for preparing this section, the following is a typical format:

Outline for an Evaluation Plan

    I. Identify the Evaluation Goals
   II. Describe the Evaluation Design
  III. Identify what will be Measured
  IV. Describe the Data Collection Plan
        A. The Indicators or Type of Data
        B. Source of the Data
        C. Data Collection Procedures
        D. Timetable
    V. Describe Sampling Plan (if applicable)
   VI. Discuss Data Analysis Techniques
  VII. Address Protection of Human Subjects and Cultural Relevancy
 VIII. Explain Staffing and Management Plans for the Evaluation
   IX. Identify Reporting Procedures
    X. Show Proposed Budget

Ethical Considerations

If you are designing a program evaluation that requests individuals share their feelings, beliefs, or other personal data beyond simple likes or dislikes, it is appropriate to ask for the consent of the individual through the use of an *informed consent* form. (Obtain consent from a parent or guardian if your client is a minor.) This consent form would itemize those things that are being requested in the evaluation such as personal data, health status including drug and alcohol history, HIV status, and so on, and then you would list any possible risk to the individual such as psychological distress at recalling events. You would provide access to counseling if need be, and someone to talk to if they have any other questions. Most of the evaluation that you will conduct in human service and educational settings will be exempt from human subject review regulations. If the evaluation has the potential to harm an individual, such as research in clinical trials and biomedical research, then it would be necessary to obtain approval for this research by application to an institutional review board (IRB) or ethical review board (ERB). Most universities have such a review board. (See Appendix D for the text of the Code of Federal Regulations that discusses who is exempt from these regulations.)

Keep your evaluation data under lock and key and have a plan to only allow authorized persons access to confidential information on clients. You must also protect client information from view of other clients, so, even as you collect data, insure that it is handled in such a way as to maintain client confidentiality.

It is also very important to consider cultural factors when developing your data collection strategies. Such factors as attitudes towards outsiders, the interpretation of the meaning of words, and mistrust or suspicion of how data will be used can affect your ability to collect the data as well as the reliability of your results. If you are designing an evaluation on an ethnic group you are not familiar with, obtain consultation or research on appropriate measures and implementation.

8

Writing the Need or Problem Statement

The Aim of the Need/Problem Statement

This chapter begins the *writing* sections of the book. As we said, we are prepping you to write a state or federal proposal complete with *Scope of Work* forms. Once you prepare a proposal in this structure, you will be able to prepare any proposal. The first part of the Request for Proposals (RFP) will ask you to submit a need statement or problem statement (or statement of need) that describes the problem and provides the rationale for the request for funding. It is often page limited to three or so pages, and it demands that you craft a succinct statement using data and other objective measures to demonstrate and substantiate the need for providing resources to address the concern.

The term *need statement* is generally used in seeking funding for programs or services, while *problem statement* usually applies to research-oriented proposals. In some professions, however, a *need* refers to the lack of access to something that is deemed desirable or fundamental to an individual or community's well-being (e.g., jobs, health care, child care). On the other hand, a *problem* refers to difficulty, trouble, or negative behavior and outcomes (e.g., drug abuse, child abuse, domestic violence). Oftentimes, the terms are used interchangeably. For our purposes, we will use the more common *need statement*, as our primary focus is on proposals written to improve conditions or address a problem existing within your community.

This section of your proposal does *not* describe your approach to address the need or problem, rather it provides a strong *rationale for why* support should be provided. The need statement is rooted in data and other factual information to understand the problem not only at the level at which you provide services, but also within the larger context of the community, state, or nation. Consider the following two examples, both seeking to offer a high school equivalency program in the community:

> There are 1,000 individuals in Agency X's service area without a high school diploma, which limits their ability to meet the labor market needs in the area.

versus

> X County has one of the lowest high school completion rates in the state ranking in the lowest third in the nation. The unemployment rate in X County of 11.4% is double the national rate. More than 1,000 individuals, or nearly 60% of the residents, ages 18–35, in the county are without a high school diploma or a job while entry-level jobs go unfilled (82% of local businesses require a high school diploma).

While the first example provided accurate information about the concerns in the service area, the second placed the needs of the service area in a broader context of the county and the nation. Thus, the funder can feel that supporting this project has a "rolling effect" by not only benefitting the community, but also improving the conditions within the county, the state, and, ultimately, the nation.

An effective need statement does five things:

1. Uses supportive evidence to clearly describe the nature and extent of the need/problem facing those you plan to serve

2. Places the nature and extent of the need/problem in a broader context than the immediate environment or setting

3. Illuminates the factors contributing to the problem or the circumstances creating the need

4. Identifies current gaps in services or programs

5. Provides a rationale for the transferability of the "promising approaches" or "best practices" to the population you seek to serve

The need statement makes clear what is occurring that requires prompt attention before conditions worsen, provides an explanation as to why the problem or need exists, and identifies some of the strategies used in other settings, such as *evidence-based practices* that have the potential for addressing the problem or need in your area. You must thoroughly understand the significance of the need/problem section as it provides the very underpinnings of the remainder of the proposal. As stated before, this section is not the place in the proposal to propose your particular "solution" or project. Rather, it lays the foundation for your particular solution to emerge as one that is responsive to the need.

The need statement provides an understanding of the impact of the problem not only on those directly affected, but also on others, including the community and/or the state and nation as a whole. A compelling case should be made as to what effect continued *non-intervention* may have on individuals, families, and the community at large. One way to make this case is to contrast the costs of prevention or timely intervention to ongoing costs of not addressing the problem (e.g., effective outcomes-based diversion programs versus incarceration). In addition, there are emotional and psychological costs to consider related to quality of life issues for the program participants and for the community (e.g., impact of being in an abusive home environment on a child's school behavior and learning).

Ideally, the need statement is comprehensive in its treatment of the problem, but not boring. Be judicious in your selection of data and use that which most pointedly tells the story of those you intend to serve. As you write the need section you want to:

- demonstrate that you have a thorough understanding of the need or problem and those you seek to serve;
- demonstrate that you are knowledgeable of the types of interventions that are successful in addressing this need or problem for your client base;
- indicate that you are aware of the multitude of barriers that may hamper the provision of service to this population;
- demonstrate that it is the same issue that the funder wants to address; and
- lay the groundwork to lead the funder to the conclusion that your approach is "client-centered" or "community-focused" and, ultimately, is one of the best possible choices to address this problem.

A Guide to Writing the Need Statement

Obviously, you cannot use all of the data you find. Scrutinize it carefully to make the best possible case for your proposal. At this point in the process, many grant writers face the mounds of data in front of them with increasing anxiety. The problem now becomes one of condensing and editing the data to make a powerful statement within a limited number of pages.

We provide the following template to help you organize your thinking. This is not meant to be your final version of the document and we are using hypothetical data for illustrative purposes. You will need to use your own data and create your own compelling statement. This will get you started.

Section One: The Nature and Extent of the Need/Problem

This section could be subtitled, "What is the problem and who is experiencing it?" In it, you will try to provide a clear picture of the incidence of the problem (e.g., the number of people per thousand in the population who experience the problem, and the rates by ethnicity, gender, age, and educational level or other pertinent demographics).

In this example, we begin with a factual opening sentence that states the topic and captures the attention of the reader. We begin to define the problem and give a percent of the total population who experiences homelessness in the geographical area to be served:

> The majority of families are only one paycheck away from homelessness and for (# *of people*) in (*your local geographic area*), this fact is all too real. The majority of homeless (defined as those without semi-permanent or permanent shelter) in (*your county*) are single mothers with children, representing the fastest growing segment of the homeless population.

The next step is to compare the local level data to the state and national data. If the incidence of the problem is greater than the state or national rates, your job is easy and your next sentence might sound like this:

> In fact, in (*year*) a total of ___ persons were homeless. The homelessness rate in (*your county*) was _____ which exceeded the state rate of ____ and the national rate of _____ in the same year (*source of data*)."

If your rate is lower than the state and national rates, study the data and see if there is a significant change in the rate in your own county from the past and you may be able to say something like this:

> Although lower than the state and national rates of ____ and ____, respectively, (*your county*) has seen a significant increase in homelessness over the past 5 years and, without intervention, will meet and exceed national rates within the next ___ years (*source of data*)."

If your rate is so low as to make your application non-competitive, you may need to find some other very unique reason as to why your community's problem is significant. For example, you may have higher crime rates than surrounding counties, or more health problems within the homeless population.

In this next paragraph, we want to know "who" is homeless in your county. What is their ethnicity? What is their educational background? Are they single persons or families? Young or old?

> In (*your county*), the rate of homelessness by ethnicity is __% white, ___% Latino, ___% African American, and ____% Asian. The rate for (*ethnic group*) is proportionately higher than all others.
>
> The average educational level for the homeless population is 10 years of schooling. The majority of homeless in our county are single African-American males (40%), followed by white males and females (30%), followed by white and African-American families (20%), and 10% Asian males and females.

You will notice that we have not made a highly emotional appeal to the funder but have already put a face on the client in the first paragraph. We feel that the funder, as well as the human service provider, is all too aware of the personal toll these problems bring. Overdramatizing the problem can work to your disadvantage.

In the above example, the data are effectively presented within the context of the community. When you place data in relationship to other data (e.g., state or national level), or other associated problems, you strengthen your request and increase the sense of urgency. For example, compare the following two statements:

> Fifty percent of the young people in the county do not graduate from high school.

versus

> Fifty percent of the young people in the county do not graduate from high school, compared to a 10% dropout rate in the state and 27% in the nation.

Section Two: Factors Contributing to the Problem or Conditions

In this section of the proposal, you will address the causes of the problem and the needs of the clients, which may stem from a variety of factors such as:

1. a lack of skill, knowledge, or awareness;

2. debilitating attitudes or harmful values;

3. physical or mental challenges and limitations;

4. dysfunctional or problem behavior;

5. limited resources or access to services;

6. institutional and systemic barriers including fragmented services; and

7. policies, practices, or laws that have negative consequences (either intended or unintended).

You want to account for each of the factors that cause the problem you are addressing. The following paragraph is a beginning to that end:

> There are a variety of conditions that may ultimately lead to homelessness. Of the homeless population, ___% have severe and persistent mental illness; ___% have experienced the loss of a job; ___% have recently divorced; and ___% have been incarcerated _____ (*source of data, year*).
>
> The top reason for job loss in the past year was personal health problems, including depression, followed by poor work performance, a lack of job-related skills, absenteeism, and health problems with other family members. In most cases, homelessness does not happen all at once. The family utilizes all available resources to maintain housing and often have one to three months of financial struggle before ending up on the streets.

It is also likely that a discussion of barriers to addressing this problem will be included in this section. For example, the stigma associated with homelessness may be so great as to cause people to delay seeking assistance, or the client's themselves may have attitudes or beliefs that prevent them from benefiting from assistance.

Each of these "causes" of the problem as stated in the above example is significant to program planning with different or complementary approaches and can be further developed along socio-economic and cultural lines, if need be. The second paragraph, which indicates that homelessness "evolves," is laying some of the groundwork necessary to support our project: early intervention to help shore up individuals to prevent impending homelessness, but, of course, we will not say anything about this in this section.

Circular Reasoning

Finally, we want to warn you about one of the most common mistakes we see in this section of the proposal which is known as *circular reasoning* (Kiritz, 1980). Circular reasoning occurs when one argues that the problem is the lack of service that one is proposing. For example, you may write in the need statement:

> The problem facing many teens is that they do not have access to a teen peer support group.

After writing this, you may proceed merrily on your way to proposing teen support groups in solution to the problem. The above statement, however, has failed to identify the needs teens have that can be met through a peer support group (e.g., loneliness, isolation, depression, etc.), and, in fact, gives the idea that the absence of a teen support group is the problem! Consider the way in which the following example might better address the needs:

> An adolescent spends an average of ___ hours per day in contact with other teens in school and afterschool activities. Research indicates that teens obtain approximately ___% of their information on drugs, sexuality, and health-related topics from their peers (*source of data, year*). From a developmental perspective, teens are moving away from parental and other adult authority and into the development of their own personal authority. In this process, teens attach to and relate best to their peers.

Thus, you have laid the groundwork for understanding the importance of a teen peer support program in addressing the developmental needs of this age group.

Section Three: Impact of the Problem

In this section, you want to look at the impact the problem has on the individual, the person's family, and the community at large. This impact can also include the benefits derived through intervention, treatment, or prevention of the problem. The following paragraphs begin this process:

> The problem of homelessness exacts a significant toll on the homeless person and family. Children who are homeless are often uprooted from their schools and their friends, suffer from poor nutrition, and lack even the most basic of

preventive care services, (e.g., immunizations). For example, 65% of school-age homeless children are without immunizations. If one is a homeless adult, one has no address or phone number to use to obtain employment.

Once an individual is homeless, the demands on community resources are great. The Government Accounting Office has estimated that it costs taxpayers approximated $35,000 per homeless family per year to provide for the family's basic needs. In a study by _____, it was shown that timely intervention targeted at a family in crisis costs approximately $15,000 per year, a savings of over half of the cost of delayed intervention! In addition to the significant financial savings, homeless children suffered less days lost from school, and improved health outcomes.

As you might have guessed, we continue to lay the groundwork for our early intervention project in response to the problem of homelessness. We want to show that our proposed project is cost effective and reduces the negative consequences associated with homelessness. *But*, we won't say anything about the proposed project in this section either.

Section Four: Promising Approaches for Improved Results

In this section, you can discuss the theoretical perspectives that have proven to be useful in designing interventions, successful approaches used in other geographic areas, and, more than likely, you will discuss the barriers to improving the problem.

Several promising strategies have been developed to address the problem of homelessness. The first is the Homeless Project based in Seattle, Washington. This project targeted a subset of homeless drug-abusing adults using the psychosocial rehabilitation approach, treatment incentives, and comprehensive services. The program helped over 67% of its participants kick the drug habit and, after a year, 87% of those were employed and paying for their own housing.

Other projects have been extremely successful in helping individuals in crisis avoid homelessness altogether. One project, in Michigan, opened a one-stop service center for struggling families. Through a combination of debt counseling, psychological services, educational remediation, job training, and health services, a full 90% of clients maintained their homes. In addition, this approach has the advantage of avoiding public resistance to a homeless shelter in the community.

You are referencing the particular theoretical and practical program components that will be effective in addressing the need/problem. This means you will demonstrate an understanding of the applicability of others' efforts in addressing the same or similar problem/need in your area. For example, psychosocial rehabilitation is named as a theoretical orientation and service component. It would be useful to briefly describe this approach, giving the success rate, treatment advantages, and cost effectiveness both at your agency and other agencies. Discuss the pros and cons of particular strategies and consider the unique needs (e.g., cultural, gender, sexual orientation, age, income, or educational level, etc.) of your participants.

Theory of Change

We feel it is important to discuss the concept of a *theory of change* as some funders may request that you state your theory of change in relation to the project you are proposing. An organization called GrantCraft outlines the difference between a logic model and theory of change:

> A theory of change takes a wide view of a desired change, carefully probing the assumptions behind each step in what may be a long and complex process. Articulating a theory of change often entails thinking through all the steps along a path toward a desired change, identifying the preconditions that will enable (and possibly inhibit) each step, listing the activities that will produce those conditions, and explaining why those activities are likely to work. It is often, but not always, presented as a flow chart.
>
> A logic model takes a more narrowly practical look at the relationship between inputs and results. It is often presented as a table listing the steps from inputs or resources through the achievement of a desired program goal. Some grant makers use separate logic models to chart the implementation components of theory of change.

(You are welcome to excerpt, copy, or quote from GrantCraft materials, with attribution to GrantCraft and inclusion of the copyright, © 2006 GrantCraft)

If you are working for a nonprofit, it is likely that the agency has developed a theory of change in relation to the problems it seeks to address within the local community. For example, another excerpt from GrantCraft states:

> Another grant maker explained the theory behind a program to improve conditions for low-income children: "The basic idea was that children do well when their families do well, and families do well when they're supported in neighborhoods, and being a supportive neighborhood means having opportunities for families to connect to economic opportunity, social networks, and

quality services and supports. . . . It was a different way to frame the problem. The problem isn't families; the problem is that families aren't connected." That insight led the foundation's program staff to ask local teams of residents to design interventions to help families connect to systems of support in their own neighborhoods. (© *2006 GrantCraft)*

Figure 8.1 summarizes the components of a theory of change.

Figure 8.1   Theory of Change

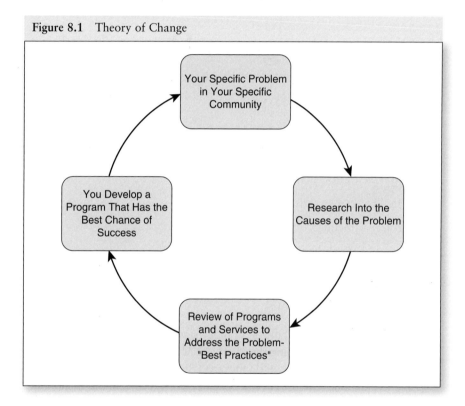

9

Program Description

The Program Description portion of many state and federal applications represents a section containing the (1) Logic Model and (2) Project Narrative (this section includes the Goals and Objectives, Implementation Activities, Timeline, and Evaluation). We also present *Scope of Work* forms in this section.

Implementation Plan

The *Implementation Plan* provides a clear account of what you plan to do, who will do it, and in what time frame the activities will be accomplished. Although we introduced this section to you in Chapter 6, we will provide you with additional examples to help you think this section through. The discussion of the implementation plan will be organized into three parts: (1) preparatory activities or inputs-resources, (2) process or specific program-related activities, and (3) units of service.

Preparatory Activities (Also Known as Inputs)

Regardless of the type of program you wish to undertake, there are a common set of activities which usually are considered at the beginning of the project. We refer to these as *preparatory activities*, that is, the start-up activities or general tasks necessary to get the program underway. (Funders usually assume that you have space to house the program you are developing. If this is not the case and you need project time to locate and secure a facility, you should include that in the preparatory activities.) With each task, it is also useful to identify the person responsible for accomplishing the activity and to estimate the time needed for completion (this will make it easier to complete a timeline). While the type of preparatory activities will vary depending upon the nature of your program, Table 9.1 lists typical activities.

Table 9.1   Preparatory Activities

Activity	Responsible Person	Time Needed
Recruit and Hire Staff and Volunteers	Executive Director/ Project Director	First Two Months
Site/Facilities and Communications	Executive Director/ Project Director	First Month
Order Special Equipment	Project Director	First Month
Obtain Program Materials	Project Director	First Two Months
Secure Interagency Agreements	Executive Director/ Project Director	First Month
Conduct Client Outreach	Project Director	First Two Months
Create Program Forms Such as HIPAA and Sign-in Sheets	Project Director	First Month
Establish Accounting and Reporting Processes	Executive Director/ Project Director	First Month
Develop Staff and Volunteer Schedules	Project Director	First Month
Set Evaluation Mechanisms	Project Director	First Month

Process- or Specific Program-Related Activities

The format for an implementation activity is, generally, who is responsible, what is to be done and by when, and how will it be evaluated. The following service topic listing itemizes some of the main activities that should be considered:

Training and Education

Examples: Community Educational Programs, School-Based Programs, or Training the Trainer Programs

1. What is the content of the presentation(s)?

2. Who will conduct the training? What criteria will be used to select and supervise trainers?

3. How will participants be recruited? How will they give consent?

4. What will be the typical format and schedule? Does it take into consideration the program participants' needs and schedule?

5. How will the services be evaluated? Will it require a special evaluation team?

Information Development and Dissemination

Examples: Ad Campaign for Drug Abuse Prevention, Video on AIDS Prevention, Health Care Newsletter, Parent Training Manual, Resource and Referral Service

1. Who is the targeted audience?

2. What is the content and format?

3. How will it be developed? Who will develop it?

4. Which group(s) will review before distribution to determine effectiveness and appropriateness?

5. What dissemination strategies will be utilized?

Counseling, Self-Efficacy and Other Support Services

Examples: Bereavement Counseling, Support Group for Victims of Abuse and Violence, Drug and Alcohol Abuse Counseling, and Crisis Hotline

1. What counseling strategies or techniques will be used?

2. What are the underlying assumptions or evidence of the validity of the techniques with the specific population?

3. What will be the counseling process and format?

4. What issues and content will be addressed?

5. What others resources (e.g., support system, professionals) will be needed by the program participants?

6. What are the plans to reduce the attrition rate?

Provision of Resources or Changing Conditions

Examples: Transportation for the Disabled, Meals Program for Older Americans, Youth Recreation Program, Health Care Screening

1. What resources will be provided?

2. What is the most effective delivery approach for the population?

3. When, where, and how will they be delivered?

4. Who will develop, organize, and deliver them?

5. Any special equipment and/or materials needed? How will these be obtained?

Units of Service (Also Known as Outputs)

In addition to identifying the tasks to be undertaken, one must also indicate *how much* of that activity will be provided. Often referred to as the *output* of your program, this question relates to the volume of work that is expected or the products of your program. It describes the types or amounts of service provided. Examples include: 100 hours of group counseling with 75 drug abuse addicts for a total of 7,500 units of service; or 150 high school drop-outs attending 10 hours of computer training sessions for a total of 1,500 units of service.

The results or outcomes are influenced by how well the program has been conceptualized and whether there were sufficient units of service to achieve the objective. It is helpful to apply a simple cost/benefit calculation. Divide the cost of the service by the units of service to see what one unit of service costs. If, for example, you find a unit of service costs very little, you should probably add more units or additional types of service under this cost center. If you find that the cost of this unit is sky high, you may need to change the service. For example, if a person can have a session with a counselor at a nonprofit agency for $50 and your cost per session worked out to be $500, it is unlikely to be funded.

The Project Narrative

This section may also be referred to in the proposal guidelines as the *Program Narrative*. It brings together your conceptualization of the work plan including the preparatory and program-related activities. Included within this section are subsections sometimes referred to as the *scope of work*, the *methods section*, or *program approach*. (If proposal instructions lack specific details about how to write this section, begin with the goal(s) of the project, followed by the objective, the implementation activities, and a detailed description of the evaluation method.) This section allows you to bring more detail into the narrative including the rationale for particular program and staffing levels, for example, than in any other section of the proposal. The following is an example of a *project narrative*:

> The "Learning for Life Project" has two goals. The first is to insure that all children receive a quality education and the second, to eliminate school dropouts. The first objective under goal one states:
>
> **Objective 1.1**: Fifty percent (50%) of two hundred (200) low-income school-age children in the XYZ School District will improve their grade level by one full level by June 30, 20xx.
>
> Implementation Activities:
>
> Children will be selected into the program based on their eligibility for federally funded lunch programs at the schools and invited to participate in the project through (1) a personal invitation to the student from the teacher, (2) a personal note to the parent(s) from the teacher, and (3) a formal letter sent to parents from the agency describing the project and obtaining consent. In-kind donations will give school supplies to participating students and parents will receive a voucher for school clothes and groceries. Approximately three cohorts of 70 students each will be enrolled into the program three times over the year.
>
> The Project Director will interview and test each of the 200 children in the first three months of the project. The results of the testing will be used to match the child with the Learning Specialist (on staff) and a tutor (the tutors will be hired to start services by month three).

Each child will receive 10 hours of targeted tutoring each week for 10 weeks. At the end of 10 weeks each student will be retested to determine any change in grade level. If 100 students have increased their grade level by one full level, the objective will be met. The Project Director will be responsible for overseeing the evaluation component.

You will continue to describe the project in this narrative format, and you may also be asked to use a scope of work form. This may seem redundant to you, and it is.

Project Timeline

In addition to describing the project activities, funders typically desire to see a schedule of those activities. A visual display of the action plan provides the reader with a real sense of when different phases of the project will be undertaken. It also helps to generate confidence in your ability to effectively plan and carry out the grant or contract requirements.

There are a variety of techniques that can be used to present the project's timetable. Table 9.2 is one of the most common timelines known as a Gantt chart. According to Wikipedia:

> A *Gantt chart* is a type of bar chart, adapted by Karol Adamiecki in 1896 and independently by Henry **Gantt** in the 1910s, that illustrates a project schedule. **Gantt charts** illustrate the start and finish dates of the terminal elements and summary elements of a project. (Gantt Chart, n.d.)

Our chart illustrates (1) the major activities and tasks, (2) the amount of time to be expended on each activity or task, and (3) the activity spread across the contract period. The time period is typically divided into months or quarters and an activity's begin and end points are depicted with row bars, Xs, or similar markings. Generally, when viewing a timeline, activities are listed in the order in which they will be accomplished (a forward sequence), as shown in Table 9.2.

By examining the project timeline, one sees which activities are to occur within a particular time frame. It is also beneficial to the project director and the staff for monitoring the completion of tasks. Some funders require quarterly reports, and from the timeline chart, they are able to determine what you plan to accomplish each quarter. It is a good idea to include the preparation of any reports to the funder as an activity on the chart.

Table 9.2 Project Timeline

Geta Grant Agency
Project "Learning for Life" Timeline
Fiscal Year July 1, 20xx to June 30, 20xx

Objective	Jul	Aug	Sep	Oct	Nov	Dec	Jan	Feb	Mar	Apr	May	Jun
Obj.1.1: 50% of 200 low-income school-age children will improve their grade level by one full level												
Send out recruitment materials	X	X				X	X	X	X			
Identify and select assessment protocols	X	X										
Assess students and pretest		X	X	X	X	X	X	X	X			
Train tutors		X	X									
Match tutors and students			X	X	X	X	X	X	X			
Conduct tutoring			X	X	X	X	X	X	X	X	X	X
Evaluation				X				X			X	X

80

If there are few activities or the project has a relatively short time span, a more condensed version of the timeline may be used (see Table 9.3).

Table 9.3   Condensed Version of Timeline

Geta Grant Agency Project "Learning for Life" Timeline Fiscal Year July 1, 20xx to June 30, 20xx	
Activity	**Time**
Hire Staff	July 1 to July 30
Train Staff and Volunteers	August 1 to September 15
Develop Curriculum and Evaluation	July 1 to September 30
Schedule Workshops	August 14 to September 30
Conduct Workshops	October 1 to May 30
Conduct Evaluation	October 1 to May 30
Prepare Final Report	June 1 to June 25

Scope of Work Forms

Many state agencies require a scope of work form that provides the basis for the legal contract. This format is useful for conceptualizing the various parts of the project for it shows the relationship between the goal, the objectives, the activities and staff responsible for the activities, a timeline, and evaluation. Of course, this is somewhat redundant to the narrative, but it does offer the advantage of a quick synopsis of each objective, implementation activity, timeline, and evaluation. The Scope of Work form in Figure 9.1 is a fairly standard form that requires an applicant to fill it out as is so recreate a matching form on your computer.

Figure 9.1 Sample Scope of Work Form

Contractor: <u>Geta Grant Agency</u>

Contract Number: _____

Agency Number: _____

Scope of Work

County: <u>Grant County</u>

The Contractor shall work toward achieving the following goals and will accomplish the following objectives. This shall be done by performing the specified activities and evaluating the results using the listed methods to focus on process or outcome.

Goal No. 1 (specify): To insure that all children receive a quality education.

Measurable Objectives	Implementation Activities	Timeline	Methods of Evaluating Process or Outcome Objectives
Obj. 1.1: Two hundred (200) low-income school-aged children will improve their grades by 20% by June 30, 20xx.	1.1 A. The educational needs of the children will be assessed. (Learning Specialist, Project Director)	7/1/xx to 11/30/xx	1.1 A. Student grade point averages will be obtained for the quarter prior to tutoring and the quarter following the end of tutoring.
	1.1 B. Assessment instruments will be reviewed and selected. (Learning Specialist)	7/1/xx to 8/31/xx	
	1.1 C. Students will be matched with tutors who will spend approx. 60 hours with them. (Project Director)	10/1/xx to 4/30/xx	If a 20% increase in grades is accomplished, the objective will be met. (Project Director, Learning Specialist)
	1.1 D. Student grade point records will be obtained for evaluation. (Project Director)	10/1/xx to 6/15/xx	

As you study the Scope of Work form, you will notice that the goal is written across the top of the page and is numbered (for example, Goal # 1). You will notice that there is also a *contract number* and *agency number* across the top right of the form. Those will be filled in by the funder if you get a contract.

The first column contains an objective that is numbered in sequence relative to the goal for which it applies. A second objective under goal one would be numbered as 1.2 and so on.

The second column identifies the implementation activities that will accomplish the particular objective. It is also customary to provide the job title of the individual(s) responsible for that activity. The numbering that we used in filling out this section is standard numbering.

The third column, the timeline column, indicates the start and end date for each activity. In most cases, you will include the year for both the start and end dates.

The final column is for the evaluation of the objective. You will state how each objective will be measured to determine if it has been achieved. It is typical to close by repeating the outcome goal, for example, if a 20% increase in grades is accomplished, the objective will be met.

There are times when you will need a second page for the same objective and you can identify it by stating: Obj 1.1 (continued) in the *measurable objective* column of the form.

10

Creating the Budget and Budget Justification

The Budget Context

There is a back-and-forth, give-and-take dance that occurs between the design of the program and the cost of the program. Making the program budget forces the grant writer to think as creatively as possible about how to deliver a meaningful and robust program at a price point that will get funded. It challenges the grant writer to think of cost-efficient ways to deliver services such as using volunteers, obtaining donations from the business community, or charging moderate fees to clients when they can afford to pay them. In the real world, it often takes many attempts to determine how best to structure the program staffing as well as the program "deliverables" to keep costs contained. One usually begins thinking about a budget as soon as the amount of funding is known and a general type of project idea becomes evident. Your thinking will be bounded by what the money can buy. Very small grants provide less room for a creative program development process to occur.

As you prepare your proposal, you are thinking of many different activities and services that will require funding to deliver. Even programs that rely heavily on volunteers have hard costs, meaning they need cold, hard cash to pay for something. As the grant writer, it will likely be up to you to pull together a budget for the project. If you are working for an agency, you will need to discuss the proposal with the executive director to see how he or she would like the budget compiled. You will most likely work with the finance director, who will work with you to learn about the project and determine what the *direct costs* of that project will be. Direct costs are those expenditures that the agency has determined are directly related to the performance of the project in some way—salaries for employees of the project, materials used in the project, rent, phones, copiers, office supplies, conferences, travel, and mileage, to name a few. (Direct costs in federal projects are subject to the allowable, allocable, and reasonable criteria as defined by the Federal Cost Principles in OMB Circular A-21.) In some agencies, direct costs may also include the time of the finance department to manage the cost center of the new project, and the time of Human Resources to hire new personnel, for example.

In most agencies, shared costs, or those that cannot be identified with a specific program, are pooled into a category known as *indirect costs*. Indirect costs generally consist of the many services the administrative branch of the agency provides such as administration, accounting, audits, certifications and review, compliance information technology, library, security, depreciation, utilities, building maintenance, and other costs usually related to the cost of business or facilities and administrative costs (F&A). The agency determines the *indirect rate* charged as a percent of each budget. For example, if the agency has a 20% indirect rate, you will include that in your budget. The finance director will most likely tell you what the agency indirect cost rate is. Some agencies have *negotiated federal rates*. This means that the agency has obtained federal government approval to charge a certain indirect rate on its contracts above the allowable indirect rate. If you are preparing a grant application that restricts the amount of indirect costs or flatly refuses these costs, you will need to include the appropriate indirect expense as direct expenses in your line-item budget. There are two ways you can do this. (1) take the percent your project represents of the total agency cost and use that percentage to get the amount attributable to your project, or (2) take the actual cost of the item.

Finally, if this proposal and budget are being prepared as part of a class assignment, you might rely on a local newspaper or Internet searches to come up with ballpark costs: salaries for employees, office space rent, and other costs such as cell phone or equipment, and set an indirect rate at the industry average for your particular industry. Human service agencies may have indirect rates of 10% to 20%, while educational institutions may have rates of 30% to 50%.

Preparation of a Line-Item Budget

A line-item budget is the most common program budget and it provides a budget "line" for each type of expenditure. The upper portion of the budget is for personnel costs and the lower portion for operating expenditures. (There is a line-item budget worksheet in Appendix D.) Table 10.1 presents your first look at a line-item, program budget.

Table 10.1   Sample Line-Item Budget

Geta Grant Agency Parenting Education Project July 1, 20xx through June 30, 20xx				
Personnel	FTE	Monthly Range (FTE)	Monthly	Yearly
Executive Director	0.1	$8,000–$10,000	$900	$10,800
Project Director	1	5,000–6,500	5,000	60,000
Educator	0.5	4,000–5,500	4,000	24,000
Therapist	0.5	4,000–5,500	4,000	24,000
Admin. Assistant	0.5	3,000–4,000	3,000	18,000
Subtotal Personnel				$136,800
Benefits @ 28%				38,304
Total Personnel				$175,104
Operating Expenses				
Communications			$400	$4,800
Rent (500 s.f. x 1.50 per s.f.)			750	9,000

Personnel	FTE	Monthly Range (FTE)	Monthly	Yearly
Office Supplies			300	3,600
Printing			200	2,400
Program Materials			300	3,600
Furniture/Fixtures			200	2,400
Equipment Purchase (computer)			100	1,200
Equipment Rental (copier)			90	1,080
Program Liability Insurance			100	1,200
Conference			350	4,200
Mileage at 0.575 (GSA rate)			120	1,440
Subtotal Operating			$2,910	$34,920
Subtotal Project Budget				$210,024
Indirect at 15% Total Budget				31,504
Grand Total				$241,528

As you study this budget, you may have noticed is that there is a column labeled "FTE" in the Personnel section of the budget. This stands for *full-time equivalent* meaning 1 FTE = a full-time employee working a 40-hour work week. You will notice that the executive director is listed as a direct personnel expenditure which means that he or she will spend 0.1 FTE of their time directly on this project in some way. (0.1 FTE = 10% of 40 hours or 4 hours a week on this project.) The third column is labeled "Monthly Range FTE" and represents the salary range a full-time employee would be paid. As you look at the column and see that the executive director has $800 per month of his or her salary paid under this contract, and it represents 10% time, so the executive director must make $8,000 a month. The agency has the monthly range for each position it manages on its "Wage and Salary

Table 10.2 Calculating FTE

FTE	Percent Time	Meaning	Hours per Year
1	100%	40 hours per week	2,080
0.8	80%	32 hours per week	1,664
0.5	50%	20 hours per week	1,040
0.25	25%	10 hours per week	520
0.10	10%	4 hours per week	208
0.05	5%	2 hours per week	104

Schedule." You would expect to hire new employees at the lowest end of the range and increase salary over time per the agency schedule. The final column represents a total for the year. (Note: 40 hours/week x % time = hours/week and 2,080 hours/year x % time = hours/year). Table 10.2 will assist you in calculating FTE.

What Does a Unit of Service Cost?

The cost of a unit of service varies based on the type of service being delivered. Generally speaking, the higher the level of professional involvement in the service delivered, the higher the cost. Medical care delivered by an M.D. costs more than that delivered by a nurse's aide, for example. For our purposes here, we are going to obtain a cost per unit of service to apply a "reasonableness" criteria to the budget; that is, does it seem reasonable to charge this amount per unit of service under our contract? And does it seem to fit within the funder's guidelines? Here's a simple example: The agency is writing a proposal to provide afterschool tutoring to 25 teens for five days a week over the 13-week spring semester. You have prepared a budget that itemizes the cost of this project, including indirect costs. You determine the project will cost $50,000 to deliver as planned. To determine cost per unit of service, we would divide $50,000 by 25 teens to arrive at cost of $2,000 per teen. If we divide this by 13 weeks, the program costs $154 per teen per week, or $30.80 per day. As this agency is providing the teens with access to credentialed teachers and teachers skilled in working with youth with learning disabilities, as well as a volunteer tutor pool and their own workbooks, the price per day is actually less than could be obtained in the community at large. Meaning, if you went into the community and tried to obtain services for one student—you found a tutor (free), bought a workbook ($75 / 65 days = $1.15/day), paid a teacher ($50/hour who spent 15 minutes a day with this student costing $12.50) and an LD specialist ($60/hour at 15 minutes = $15), rented a site ($100/day x 65 days = $6,500 / 12 is $541.66 per student / 65 days = $8.33/day), and add staff time to obtain and supervise these services at $32 per hour, 3 hours per day ($96 / 12 = $8/day) for a total of $45. It is clear you would not be able to procure this for $30.80 per day. This example meets the reasonableness criteria.

Personnel expenditures are generally the largest percentage of costs of a project. Table 10.3 shows the common types of personnel expenditures in program budgets and can be used by you in planning the budget.

Table 10.3   Common Personnel Expenditures

Executive Director	Finance Director	Human Resources
Project Director	Project Professional Staff	Project Clerical Staff
Payroll Taxes	Clinical Supervision	Employee Health Benefits
Information Technology	Student Interns	Receptionist

What kind of staff do you need to run the project? In almost all cases, there will some combination of the following staffing configuration:

1. A project director who will have overall administrative responsibility for the project and some direct service responsibilities. This individual has the educational background and experience to manage this type of program. In most cases, funders will look for a full-time person in this role, and the agency will depend upon this person to implement the project and follow the budget as approved. The project director will often be responsible to deliver some of the services while managing the project as a whole.

2. The professional staff whose education and expertise anchor the service delivery component of the program. These are the people who deliver the service. Perhaps they will be licensed therapists, counselors, child care providers, credentialed educators, or health care providers.

3. Volunteers may also be used to deliver services. Perhaps the volunteers will be professionals, paraprofessionals, students, or general community members. Volunteers provide services under the contract for free. This level

of staffing often requires a level of recruitment into the project, a training program to prepare them for the delivery of services (and this training should be included in the program design and costs) and supervision. Using interns or volunteers in a project is usually a cost-effective manner to deliver services and contributes to the field as a whole as it builds the capacity of future professionals.

4. Clerical/administrative assistants/receptionists are persons hired to manage phones, paperwork, scheduling, data entry, and other clerical duties for the project.

5. Finance director and accounting staff to establish a cost center for the project, manage the project's finances, pay bills and track expenditures, and prepare financial reports.

6. A percentage of time of the executive director to provide supervision to the project director, interact with the funder to negotiate or implement the contract, and to ensure fiscal and programmatic compliance. Some projects also include a percentage of the executive director's time to attend community meetings or conduct other public relations efforts of the project.

7. Human resources director to recruit open positions for the project and provide staff training.

Employee benefits are also included under "Personnel Costs." The agency will determine what is included in this benefits line. At a minimum, this amount will include employer contributions for federal and state governments (for example, FICA and Federal Withholding taxes, State Disability Insurance, Medicare, and Social Security contributions). Other employee benefits provided by the employer may also be included on this line and will often include health and dental insurance and retirement funds. The total amount of payroll taxes and benefits provided to the employee is calculated as a percentage of the total salary amount. The benefit amount will vary widely depending on the organization type—many nonprofit social service agencies have benefits calculated closer to 20% to 25% while governmental organizations or institutions of higher education may assess benefits up to 30% to 50%.

Now let us look at the second section of the budget that addresses operating expenses. Again, it is important to look carefully at the proposal itself and identify all of the items that will cost money. The operating costs listed in Table 10.4 are typical among project proposals.

You will probably notice that we have included consultants in the operating budget and not the personnel budget. In most cases, consultants will be

Table 10.4   Common Operational Costs

Rent	Utilities	Printing
Office Supplies	Equipment Rental	Equipment Purchase
Communications	Staff Training	Project Materials
Project Liability Insurance	Advertising	Travel
Consultants	Conferences	Mileage

included under operating budgets as a non-employee program expenditure. (We would classify a consultant as a non-employee as they work independently under a consultant contract, are responsible to carry their own liability insurance and health insurance plans, and pay their own taxes on income they make.) In addition, many state and federal funders have established fixed reimbursement rates for such things as mileage, per diem for travel, and consultants, and you will want to carefully read the application for detailed descriptions of what is acceptable. Perhaps other details in the budget will not be apparent until you reach the negotiation stage. For example, you might have $5,000 in the budget to purchase a computer and printer, and during the negotiation, the funder tells you that they will not pay for the purchase of equipment, but will allow you to rent it; you can then make the necessary adjustments. *Read* all of the instructions the funder gives on preparing the budget. Most funders state their restrictions in their application package.

Budget Justifications

In addition to writing the line-item budget, many funders want you to provide a detailed narrative on the budget and drill down to what is included on each line and how the totals per line were reached. In a budget justification, each of the lines is explained. The following is an example of a budget justification for the line-item budget presented in Table 10.1:

Budget Justification for Geta Grant Agency

Personnel

Executive Director: The agency executive director will be responsible for the supervision of the project director, a small part of community networking, attending the funder's yearly conference, and providing overall program fiscal and operational compliance representing 4 hours a week of her time (.05 FTE), for a total of $9,600 a year.

Project Director: A Project Director will work full-time (100%) on this project with program implementation and evaluation responsibilities, staff and volunteer supervision, and report-writing duties. The project director who is also a licensed marriage and family therapist, will also provide 10 hours a week of direct service under this contract. The salary is $57,600 per year.

Educator: An Educator will work full-time to conduct educational evaluations, create specialized learning plans, and conduct one-on-one and group educational programs for the duration of the project for a total of $38,400 per year.

Therapist: A part-time (50% time) therapist will work with the most troubled youth and their parents in in-depth conducting sessions at the program site and work in coordination with the child's teacher and probation officer for a total of $24,000.

Administrative Assistant: An administrative assistant will be assigned 50% time on this project to prepare project correspondence, receive phone calls from interested parents, schedule programs and respond to questions or requests for information at a total of $21,600 per year.

The Subtotal Personnel is $146,400.

Employee benefits have been calculated at 25%, which includes FICA and Federal Withholding, SDI, State Withholding, Medicare, Worker's Compensation and Health, Vision, and Dental Benefits. The total benefits for this project is $48,960.

Total Personnel Costs are $183,000.

Operating Expenses

- Communications has been calculated at $500/month to include $180/month for three land-line phones in the office; $60 per month for 3 cell phones for the project director, educator, and therapist so that they are available during and after work hours, usage $70; and Internet connection $70 for a total of $6,000 per year.
- Rent has been calculated at $1.50 per square foot times 500 square feet of space for a total of $750 per month times 12 months totaling $9,000. Utilities are included in rent pricing.
- Office Supplies are $400 per month and include 6-part file folders on each participant, notebooks, locking tote boxes to transport files between sites, paper, pens, copier toner, printer ink, desk supplies, phone supplies, and receipt books for a total of $4,800/year.

- Travel expenses include mileage to and from school sites, homes, and community meeting places for an estimated 100 miles per staff, or 300 miles per month at 45 cents per mile times 12 months for a total of $1,620 per year. Also included in travel is $852 per person, for transportation, and per diem (at State Board of Control rates) to one major conference for two staff members. The total request for travel is $3,324.
- Printing is calculated at $150/month to provide worksheets for the youth classroom exercises, announcements for students and parents, the monthly newsletter, and parenting newsletters throughout the year for a yearly total of $1,800.
- Vehicle Lease: The vehicle (small bus) will be leased for a total of 8 trips at $450/trip for a total of $3,600. The vehicle will be used to transport students and faculty on educational field trips. The cost of the vehicle includes insurance and a driver with a Class B license.
- Insurance (auto) includes an additional $75 per trip to provide student and faculty health insurance riders and coverage of their belongings for a total of $600 a year.
- Insurance Liability: General liability coverage for the program for all students, staff, volunteers, and guests on the premises at $200/month or $2,400 a year.
- Client Incentives are used to reward students who are climbing the ladder to success. Students will receive back packs, iPods, and educational games for a total of $1,800 per year.
- Educational Materials purchases text books, curriculum units for the Educator, and materials that the Therapist needs to work effectively with the children at $400/month for a total of $4,800/year.
- Furniture includes desks, bookcases, tables, and chairs at $300/month or a total of $3,600/year.
- Equipment Rental applies to the copier lease at $400/month. The lease includes copier maintenance quarterly for a total of $4,800/year.
- Equipment Purchase includes the purchase of three iPads to be used by the Educator, Therapist, and Project Director for a total of $1,500 and one desktop computer at $300 for the Administrative Assistant for a total of $1,800.

The Total Operating Costs are $48,324.

- Indirect Costs are charged to this project at 15% of the project total $266,023 at $34,699 to provide reimbursement for administrative overhead for the project.

The Total Budget for this project is $266,023.

Other Types of Budgets

Some foundations and nonprofit trusts require a more simplified budget in which you indicate expense categories rather than itemizing line by line. The budget in Table 10.5 places line-item categories into more general categories. This type of budget provides the agency with much more flexibility in the actual allocation of expenses, and it is usually possible for the agency to transfer funds between lines without contacting the funder.

Table 10.5   Simplified Budget

Geta Grant Agency Parenting Education Project Budget July 1, 20xx through June 30, 20xx	
Personnel	
Salaries	$136,800
Benefits @ 28%	38,304
Subtotal Personnel	$175,104
Operating Expenses	
Overhead	$31,504
Program	29,280
Travel and Conferences	5,640
Subtotal Operating Expenses	$66,424
Total Budget Request	$241,528

Matching Funds and In-Kind Budgets

When some of the costs of the project will be assumed by the agency, the agency is said to be contributing this money *in-kind*, and this portion of agency-borne expense is indicated in the budget. The funding for an in-kind contribution may come from the agency's fundraising efforts, from other funding sources that are devoted to these services, through the receipt of product and services from the community, and through its use of volunteers allowing it to reduce costs.

Other funding sources may require that the agency provide *matching funds* of a certain percent of the amount requested. For example, one state office offered to fund 75% of the cost of providing a case management system to pregnant and parenting teens and required the applicant to provide a 25% match. An agency needs to determine what existing funds can be used to provide a match in this contract, or develop a way to bring in additional funds to meet the match. In both cases, whether *in-kind* or *matching funds*, the funder expects that it will receive full credit for the number of clients to be served under the project and that the clients should not be "double counted" for services elsewhere. In other words, you can't count clients whose service is fully funded under one contract to meet the goals of another contract.

The example in Table 10.6 indicates one way to present an in-kind budget. The first column indicates the funder's portion of the total request, the second column indicates the agency's portion, and the third column indicates the total to be allocated for each item. Note: A similar format can be used if you are writing a proposal in which the resources are coming from more than one funder. Indicate the source of the funding in each column, followed by a total funding column.

As you may also be interested in applying for federal funding, we have included a copy of the budget used in federal proposals in the table at the end of the chapter.

Table 10.6   In-Kind Budget

Geta Grant Agency Budget Request July 1, 20xx to June 30, 20xx					
Personnel	FTE	Yearly Salary	Funding Request	Agency In-Kind	Total
Executive Director	.05	$60,000	$2,000	$1,000	$3,000
Project Director	1.0	42,000	38,000	4,000	42,000
Clerical	.50	25,044	12,522	0	12,522
Accounting	.10	48,000	0	4,800	4,800
Subtotal Salaries			$52,522	$9,800	$62,322
Benefits @ 20%			10,504	1,960	12,464
Total Personnel			$63,026	$11,760	$74,786

(Continued)

Table 10.6   (Continued)

Personnel	FTE	Yearly Salary	Funding Request	Agency In-Kind	Total
Operating Expenses					
Rent			4,000	5,360	$9,360
Office Supplies			1,500	300	1,800
Printing			2,200	600	2,800
Equipment Rent/ Maint			2,800	400	3,200
Telephone			2,000	400	2,400
Travel			2,000	580	2,580
Subtotal Operating			$14,500	$7,640	$22,140
Total Budget Request			$77,526	$19,400	$96,926

Other Budgeting Issues

Budget Adjustment

At times during the contract year, changes may need to be made in the budget. These changes may be due to a desire to reallocate savings in one area to cover overages in another. Some funders will allow for a transfer between line items to a small extent without their approval, but, in most cases, the funder wants to ensure the integrity of the proposed services if there are significant changes in funding. This process of requesting a transfer between lines is called a *budget adjustment*.

As you will see in Table 10.7, one column lists the current contract totals for the year, another indicates the amount of money you want to add or subtract from the column, and the final column indicates the new totals. With budget adjustments, you are not changing the total amount that you have to work with, just reallocating the money between lines.

The adjusted budget will most often need to have a written explanation attached, which describes what has happened, on a per line basis, to necessitate the request for a change.

Table 10.7 Budget Adjustment

	Prior Approved Amount	Adjustment Effective 10/1/20xx	New Approved Amount
Personnel			
Executive Director	$2,000	(100)	$1,900
Project Director	38,000	0	38,000
Clerical	12,522	0	12,522
Benefits	10,504	(20)	10,484
Total Personnel	$52,522	(120)	$52,502
Operating Expenses			
Rent	$4,000	0	$4,000
Office Supplies	1,500	500	2,000
Printing	2,200	(380)	1,820
Equipment Rental Maintenance	2,800	(500)	2,300
Telephone	2,000	0	2,000
Travel	2,000	500	2,500
Subtotal Operating	14,500	120	14,500
Total Budget	$77,526	0	$77,526

Budget Amendment

If, during the course of the contract, your scope of work has been expanded or reduced, you may need to do a budget amendment reflecting this change. A simple way to think about this is: When you need to shift money and it does not alter the scope of work in any way, you write an adjustment. If something has happened to significantly alter the scope, for example, the funder has asked you to take on an additional project or activity and will provide more money, you will write an amendment. Some funders require an amendment if you are seeking to move more than $5,000 (or some other predetermined amount). Amendments are usually written using the same budget format for requesting adjustments.

The major difference between an amendment and an adjustment is that the amendment changes your contract with the funder and goes through a formal approval process. You will receive a new copy of the contract with the amended budget and any program changes resulting from the amendment.

Contract Negotiations and Subcontracting

It will be a good day when the agency is notified that the proposal has been approved for funding. If the funding is less than requested, you will most likely reconvene with the team to discuss the changes that will need to be made to the budget and program. As the grant writer, you are in a key position to know how the budget impacts the program and vice versa. Be conscious of the possible "domino" effect that a change in the budget will have on the entire program and develop a couple of possible changes to the proposal that will meet the funder's request. Discuss these changes with your team and prepare to (1) attend the contract negotiation session or (2) submit the changes to the funder directly.

If there is a formal contract negotiation, you, and most likely the agency executive director, will meet face-to-face with the funder, review what is going to be provided by the contract, review the changes that reduced funding has made to the proposal, and answer other questions the funder may have. The funder may want to ask questions about the project or make changes to the project. Always approach these negotiations carefully, as it can be very easy to make changes in a project that will be very difficult to live with.

No one knows the project better than you. Approach the negotiations from the perspective of win-win. The funder wants a good program just as you do. Here are a few guidelines for negotiating contracts:

1. Re-read the proposal just prior to going into the negotiations. Be intimately familiar with all of it just as you were when writing it 6 months ago.

2. Create an atmosphere of partnership with the contract negotiator.

3. Take your time when you make changes. Look at the impact any change will have on the objectives even if this means that you ask for additional time to consider the impact of the requested changes on the project.

4. Be prepared to discuss your rationale for keeping the project as initially developed in the proposal, and don't be too anxious to change it.

5. If the agency has not been awarded the full amount requested, prepare a new version of the proposal in advance of the meeting. This enables you to have time to re-think the budget and program, and decide upon the revisions that make the most sense to you.

6. Remember to maintain your integrity. If you know that the agency cannot do the job for the amount of money offered, say so. In this case, the agency will need to decide if it is worth pursuing. It is possible, and we have seen it happen, that the agency will choose to turn down the contract because accepting it would be too costly to the agency.

Subcontracting

Subcontracting means that your agency receives the master contract from the funder. This makes your agency the primary contractor or the "lead agency." The lead agency then prepares *subcontracts* for the other agency involved in the project. This is a typical arrangement used by a collaborative or by two or more community agencies in partnership. The subcontracting agency is bound by the same contractual terms as the primary contractor. The primary contractor is responsible for ensuring that the subcontracting agency abides by the terms of the contract and usually prepares a legally binding agreement to this effect. (For a more in-depth treatment of the topic of contracts and subcontracting, see Kettner, Maroney, & Martin, 2008.)

If you are using subcontractors, you have to address this issue within the body of the grant itself in order to clearly identify by objectives the role of the subcontractor in the contract, and to establish the credibility of the subcontractor in the applicant capability section. The budget of the subcontractor is included in the main budget and fully described in the budget justification.

As you review the steps in budget preparation, you can see why this should not be left to the last minute. Preparing the budget requires that you have a thorough grasp of the project, including all of the details of the implementation activities, so that you can be certain not to omit any major costs. *Remember: Changes in the program will have an impact on the budget, and changes in the budget will have an impact on the program.*

Federal Proposal Budget Forms

BUDGET INFORMATION - Non-Construction Programs

OMB Approval No. 0348-0044

SECTION A - BUDGET SUMMARY

Grant Program Function or Activity (a)	Catalog of Federal Domestic Assistance Number (b)	Estimated Unobligated Funds		New or Revised Budget		
		Federal (c)	Non-Federal (d)	Federal (e)	Non-Federal (f)	Total (g)
1.		$	$	$	$	$
2.						
3.						
4.						
5. Totals		$	$	$	$	$

SECTION B - BUDGET CATEGORIES

6. Object Class Categories	GRANT PROGRAM, FUNCTION OR ACTIVITY				Total
	(1)	(2)	(3)	(4)	(5)
a. Personnel	$	$	$	$	$
b. Fringe Benefits					
c. Travel					
d. Equipment					
e. Supplies					
f. Contractual					
g. Construction					
h. Other					
i. Total Direct Charges (sum of 6a-6h)					
j. Indirect Charges					
k. TOTALS (sum of 6i and 6j)	$	$	$	$	$
7. Program Income	$	$	$	$	$

Authorized for Local Reproduction

Previous Edition Usable

Standard Form 424A (Rev. 7-97)
Prescribed by OMB Circular A-102

SECTION C - NON-FEDERAL RESOURCES

(a) Grant Program	(b) Applicant	(c) State	(d) Other Sources	(e) TOTALS
8.	$	$	$	$
9.				
10.				
11.				
12. TOTAL *(sum of lines 8-11)*	$	$	$	$

SECTION D - FORECASTED CASH NEEDS

	Total for 1st Year	1st Quarter	2nd Quarter	3rd Quarter	4th Quarter
13. Federal	$	$	$	$	$
14. Non-Federal					
15. TOTAL *(sum of lines 13 and 14)*	$	$	$	$	$

SECTION E - BUDGET ESTIMATES OF FEDERAL FUNDS NEEDED FOR BALANCE OF THE PROJECT

(a) Grant Program	FUTURE FUNDING PERIODS (Years)			
	(b) First	(c) Second	(d) Third	(e) Fourth
16.	$	$	$	$
17.				
18.				
19.				
20. TOTAL *(sum of lines 16-19)*	$	$	$	$

SECTION F - OTHER BUDGET INFORMATION

21. Direct Charges:	22. Indirect Charges:

23. Remarks:

Authorized for Local Reproduction   Standard Form 424A (Rev. 7-97) Page 2

(Continued)

(Continued)

INSTRUCTIONS FOR THE SF-424A

Public reporting burden for this collection of information is estimated to average 180 minutes per response, including time for reviewing instructions, searching existing data sources, gathering and maintaining the data needed, and completing and reviewing the collection of information. Send comments regarding the burden estimate or any other aspect of this collection of information, including suggestions for reducing this burden, to the Office of Management and Budget, Paperwork Reduction Project (0348-0044), Washington, DC 20503.

PLEASE DO NOT RETURN YOUR COMPLETED FORM TO THE OFFICE OF MANAGEMENT AND BUDGET. SEND IT TO THE ADDRESS PROVIDED BY THE SPONSORING AGENCY.

General Instructions

This form is designed so that application can be made for funds from one or more grant programs. In preparing the budget, adhere to any existing Federal grantor agency guidelines which prescribe how and whether budgeted amounts should be separately shown for different functions or activities within the program. For some programs, grantor agencies may require budgets to be separately shown by function or activity. For other programs, grantor agencies may require a breakdown by function or activity. Sections A, B, C, and D should include budget estimates for the whole project except when applying for assistance which requires Federal authorization in annual or other funding period increments. In the latter case, Sections A, B, C, and D should provide the budget for the first budget period (usually a year) and Section E should present the need for Federal assistance in the subsequent budget periods. All applications should contain a breakdown by the object class categories shown in Lines a-k of Section B.

Section A. Budget Summary Lines 1-4 Columns (a) and (b)

For applications pertaining to a *single* Federal grant program (Federal Domestic Assistance Catalog number) and *not requiring* a functional or activity breakdown, enter on Line 1 under Column (a) the Catalog program title and the Catalog number in Column (b).

For applications pertaining to a *single* program *requiring* budget amounts by multiple functions or activities, enter the name of each activity or function on each line in Column (a), and enter the Catalog number in Column (b). For applications pertaining to multiple programs where none of the programs require a breakdown by function or activity, enter the Catalog program title on each line in Column (a) and the respective Catalog number on each line in Column (b).

For applications pertaining to *multiple* programs where one or more programs *require* a breakdown by function or activity, prepare a separate sheet for each program requiring the breakdown. Additional sheets should be used when one form does not provide adequate space for all breakdown of data required. However, when more than one sheet is used, the first page should provide the summary totals by programs.

Lines 1-4, Columns (c) through (g)

For new applications, leave Column (c) and (d) blank. For each line entry in Columns (a) and (b), enter in Columns (e), (f), and (g) the appropriate amounts of funds needed to support the project for the first funding period (usually a year).

For continuing grant program applications, submit these forms before the end of each funding period as required by the grantor agency. Enter in Columns (c) and (d) the estimated amounts of funds which will remain unobligated at the end of the grant funding period only if the Federal grantor agency instructions provide for this. Otherwise, leave these columns blank. Enter in columns (e) and (f) the amounts of funds needed for the upcoming period. The amount(s) in Column (g) should be the sum of amounts in Columns (e) and (f).

For supplemental grants and changes to existing grants, do not use Columns (c) and (d). Enter in Column (e) the amount of the increase or decrease of Federal funds and enter in Column (f) the amount of the increase or decrease of non-Federal funds. In Column (g) enter the new total budgeted amount (Federal and non-Federal) which includes the total previous authorized budgeted amounts plus or minus, as appropriate, the amounts shown in Columns (e) and (f). The amount(s) in Column (g) should not equal the sum of amounts in Columns (e) and (f).

Line 5 - Show the totals for all columns used.

Section B Budget Categories

In the column headings (1) through (4), enter the titles of the same programs, functions, and activities shown on Lines 1-4, Column (a), Section A. When additional sheets are prepared for Section A, provide similar column headings on each sheet. For each program, function or activity, fill in the total requirements for funds (both Federal and non-Federal) by object class categories.

Line 6a-i - Show the totals of Lines 6a to 6h in each column.

Line 6j - Show the amount of indirect cost.

Line 6k - Enter the total of amounts on Lines 6i and 6j. For all applications for new grants and continuation grants the total amount in column (5), Line 6k, should be the same as the total amount shown in Section A, Column (g), Line 5. For supplemental grants and changes to grants, the total amount of the increase or decrease as shown in Columns (1)-(4), Line 6k should be the same as the sum of the amounts in Section A, Columns (e) and (f) on Line 5.

Line 7 - Enter the estimated amount of income, if any, expected to be generated from this project. Do not add or subtract this amount from the total project amount, Show under the program

INSTRUCTIONS FOR THE SF-424A (continued)

narrative statement the nature and source of income. The estimated amount of program income may be considered by the Federal grantor agency in determining the total amount of the grant.

Section C. Non-Federal Resources

Lines 8-11 Enter amounts of non-Federal resources that will be used on the grant. If in-kind contributions are included, provide a brief explanation on a separate sheet.

> **Column (a)** - Enter the program titles identical to Column (a), Section A. A breakdown by function or activity is not necessary.

> **Column (b)** - Enter the contribution to be made by the applicant.

> **Column (c)** - Enter the amount of the State's cash and in-kind contribution if the applicant is not a State or State agency. Applicants which are a State or State agency should leave this column blank.

> **Column (d)** - Enter the amount of cash and in-kind contributions to be made from all other sources.

> **Column (e)** - Enter totals of Columns (b), (c), and (d).

Line 12 - Enter the total for each of Columns (b)-(e). The amount in Column (e) should be equal to the amount on Line 5, Column (f), Section A.

Section D. Forecasted Cash Needs

Line 13 - Enter the amount of cash needed by quarter from the grantor agency during the first year.

Line 14 - Enter the amount of cash from all other sources needed by quarter during the first year.

Line 15 - Enter the totals of amounts on Lines 13 and 14.

Section E. Budget Estimates of Federal Funds Needed for Balance of the Project

Lines 16-19 - Enter in Column (a) the same grant program titles shown in Column (a), Section A. A breakdown by function or activity is not necessary. For new applications and continuation grant applications, enter in the proper columns amounts of Federal funds which will be needed to complete the program or project over the succeeding funding periods (usually in years). This section need not be completed for revisions (amendments, changes, or supplements) to funds for the current year of existing grants.

If more than four lines are needed to list the program titles, submit additional schedules as necessary.

Line 20 - Enter the total for each of the Columns (b)-(e). When additional schedules are prepared for this Section, annotate accordingly and show the overall totals on this line.

Section F. Other Budget Information

Line 21 - Use this space to explain amounts for individual direct object class cost categories that may appear to be out of the ordinary or to explain the details as required by the Federal grantor agency.

Line 22 - Enter the type of indirect rate (provisional, predetermined, final or fixed) that will be in effect during the funding period, the estimated amount of the base to which the rate is applied, and the total indirect expense.

Line 23 - Provide any other explanations or comments deemed necessary.

11

Other Proposal Components and Finishing Touches

This chapter provides an overview of what some refer to as the *finishing touches* of the proposal. These are the items that complete the proposal and are often prepared after the main sections have been written. You will want to follow the funder's guidelines regarding what items are requested and acceptable to attach to the proposal in an appendix, and often these include the following:

1. Project Abstract

2. Agency Capability Statement

3. Letters of Support

4. Developing the Memorandum of Understanding (MOU)

5. Documents to be attached: List of board members, audited financial statements, current budget, organizational chart, the agency IRS 501(c)(3) letter.

As you near the home stretch of proposal preparation there are some very important "last" pieces that become part of the proposal document. We address those components with examples in the following discussion.

Project Abstract

Most funders will ask for a 100-word abstract (or some other limited statement) of the proposed project. This will be used to briefly describe the proposal to reviewers, or to develop a press release on the project. It is important to give this abstract a lot of thought. It should capture the detail of the project about who is being served and what services will be delivered. Here is an example:

Project Abstract

The Share Ourselves Agency proposes two of the highest priority projects selected by 200 parents in the target area. Project One provides a dental clinic at each elementary school in the Auburn area, providing cleaning, screening, and hygiene kits to 800 children and fillings to a total of 400 low-income school-aged children. Project Two targets 40 high-risk adolescents to receive educational assessments, and 40 hours of need-specific tutoring after school to raise their performance by one full grade level. Both projects will utilize 30 volunteers working with professional staff to deliver services. The budget request is $185,000.

Agency Capability Statement

Almost all proposals require an agency capability statement (or applicant capability statement). In this statement, the agency presents its history and qualifications to the funder. Now that you understand the history and mission of the agency, as well as some of its program offerings of the present and past, it is a good time to start writing the agency capability statement. Of course, you will need to fine tune this statement once the entire proposal is completed to insure that you have highlighted the appropriate agency experience and described the current proposal accurately.

The agency capability statement establishes an organization's credibility to successfully undertake the project. It indicates who is applying for the grant, what qualifies an agency to conduct the project, and what resources, (for example, organizational, community) are available to support the effort. This section helps establish and generate confidence that the agency is programmatically and financially competent and qualified to address the problem.

In developing this section, the grant writer reflects the agency's image of itself as well as the constituency's image of it. This includes describing the organization's unique contributions to those it serves and capturing the community's regard for these contributions. When preparing this section, one should provide quantitative evidence of the agency's accomplishments. A recurring weakness in capability statements is observed when the agency makes qualitative assessments of the organization without some corroborating data to support the claims.

A capability statement should accomplish two things: (1) it should describe the agency's characteristics and its track record, and (2) it should demonstrate how those qualities make them qualified to undertake the proposed project. Many times, grant writers accomplish the first task but leave it up to the reviewers to infer the latter. They often fail to present a cogent argument that connects what they have done with what they are now proposing to do.

When writing this section, avoid overusing the words *we* and *our*. It is appropriate to refer to the name of the agency or simply write *the agency* throughout the text. Write as if you are developing a public relations article for a national newsletter, informing the reader, making it interesting, but brief.

When you are serving as a lead agency for a collaborative effort, you would highlight your agency's experience and also include subsections for each of the other agencies involved. It is customary to ask the participating agency to write their own capability sections to include in the proposal. A typical agency capability statement will reflect much of the following information:

(1) *Mission of the Agency*—the overall philosophy and aims of the organization and vision for the agency

(2) *History of the Agency*—a brief overview of when, why, and how the agency started, and whether its focus has changed over time.

(3) *Organizational Resources*—a description of the agency's funding track record and of the human and material resources available to this project. (Include the pertinent background of staff, especially expertise in areas related to the

need/problem, other professionals associated with the agency, and any special equipment, materials, and services which can support the proposed project.)

(4) *Community Recognition and Support*—an indication of how the agency is regarded, including awards, accreditations, and honors bestowed upon it and the staff, as well as how the community is involved in the agency's operation and structure (for example, through membership, in programs, on committees, and boards).

(5) *Interagency Collaboration and Linkages*—a depiction of the linkages and support available from other organizations that can assist with the proposed project, including memberships in local, state, and national networks.

(6) *Agency Programs*—an overview of the unique programmatic contributions the agency makes to its clients and the community, including the aims and types of programs, and a quantitative picture of what is accomplished (for example, the numbers served, the distribution rate of materials, the cost savings resulting from these services, and program outcomes).

(7) *Agency Strengths*—a description of the organizational characteristics that make the agency particularly suited to implement the project. In general, you indicate what is being proposed and how that fits with what the organization already has accomplished. For example, the agency may already be serving the target group, or addressing the need/problem, or using a particular technique or strategy that it now wishes to modify or implement in a different manner. Provide the agency web address somewhere in the agency capability statement.

Sample Agency Capability Statement

The nationally recognized and regionally acclaimed Boys and Girls Clubs of Nirvana has provided 38 years of service to youth in the greater Nirvana area. The mission of the agency is to "improve the physical well-being and quality of life for boys and girls living in Nirvana." The agency's staff of 15 youth workers, seven area managers, and executive director have offered programs to over 1,200 youth per year. In addition, the agency has over 40 volunteer tutors who provide at least five hours a week each of service to the youth.

Boys and Girls Clubs of Nirvana partner with several other community youth-serving organizations: the LookOut, Okay to Learn School, and Happy Kickers link with the agency to expand and enhance program offerings. Current programs offered by the agency include afterschool tutoring, physical education programs, and nutrition programs to help youth overcome the impact of poverty on their lives. Program outcomes indicate that 89% of the youth in the agency's programs have improved their grades by at least one full grade level, and 92% have improved their overall fitness ranking by one full level after participating in the program. These outstanding results help guarantee the youth will progress satisfactorily through school and be prepared for a healthy future. (More program information can be found on our website at www.boysandgirlsclub .org.)

The proposed program targets extremely high-risk youth and mobilizes services for them and their parents. The project will provide 100 families with increased nutritional support through donations from xxx Grocery Store distributed by the agency, tutoring services five days a week, and a family ombudsman who makes weekly visits to assist the family to obtain needed services.

The Boys and Girls Club of Nirvana are prepared to conscientiously address the multiple problems faced by needy families in Nirvana and have received the prestigious County of Nirvana Supervisor's Award, the State of Nirvana's Youth Angel Award, and the National Best Boy's and Girl's Club Award. Program staff have the expertise and experience to build the required relationships with youth and their families. One of the parents served says, "Boys and Girls Club of Nirvana has helped my children learn. They get better grades at school now. They help me feel more comfortable to talk to the teachers. I am happy they are here!"

Letters of Support

Letters of support are usually obtained from other agencies, possible clients, and influential community members including elected officials. It is most usual to make contact with the potential letter writer by phone, explain the project, and ascertain their willingness to write a letter of support. If the response is positive, fax or e-mail a sample letter to them that contains enough details about the project that they can write their letter from it, or simply copy your letter onto their letterhead and sign it. You will also provide the writer with directions as to when the letter is due and how you want to receive the letter—are you going to pick it up, have it mailed to you, or have it faxed to you? Below is a sample of a request for a letter of support:

Sample Letter of Support

Dear Agency Executive Director:

The Geta Grant agency is applying for $100,000 in funding to the Office of Health and Human Services to fund a case management system for the Families

First Collaborative. This project, called "Management for Health" provides a full-time caseworker to address the mental health, educational, parenting, employment, housing, food, and health needs of the highest-risk Latino and white families in the cities of Lemon, Tangerine, and Banana. We expect that over 200 families with multiple needs will be served in the first year. In addition, our project will evaluate the effectiveness of case management on health and mental health outcomes with this population.

Agencies included in this collaborative proposal include the Department of Education, A Fine Health Center, the Mental Health Center, the Human Interaction Commission, Housing First, and the Food Bank Distribution Center.

If you see the need for these services in our community, or if you are willing to partner with us in this proposal to provide X, Y, and Z, please write a letter of support addressed to: Mary Smith, Program Officer, Office of Health and Human Services, Department 007, 200 State Lane, Room 123, Our Town, CA 90009 but, if you are mailing the support letter please send the letter to me at: Mary Grant Writer, Geta Grant Agency, 1111 One Street, This Town, CA 90002. We thank you for your support.

Please call us to pick up the letter by Friday, June 2, 20xx.

Sincerely,

Mary Grant Writer, Project Director

As the grant writer, be prepared to make follow-up phone calls to the agencies to encourage their completion of the letter, answer any questions they may have, and to schedule a time to pick up the letter if you are nearing the proposal deadline. It is wise to request the letters early, as you are preparing the other sections of the proposal, to avoid the delay as the proposal deadline approaches. In some instances, you may be asked by the organizations to draft a letter of support for them. This is often ideal as you can be very specific about the items you want emphasized by each supporting source.

Memorandum of Understanding (MOU)

The role of any subcontractor under the lead agency should be spelled out in a written agreement. The *Memorandum of Understanding* (MOU—with each letter pronounced separately) is a formal quasi-legal document that itemizes what each of the parties will do and their relationship to each other and the funder.

The following is an example of an MOU:

Memorandum of Understanding

This Memorandum of Understanding is entered into on _____ by the Geta Grant Agency, hereafter, the lead agency, and the Boys and Girls Club of Grant City, hereafter, the subcontractor. Funding for this project is provided by the U. S. Department of Health Services under what is to be called the master contract and all parties are responsible to insure that terms and services are delivered and met as required in the master contract. Funding is contingent upon the continuation of funding through the U.S. Department of Health Services and conditional upon continuation of said funding.

The term of this MOU is from _____ to _____. The subcontractor can submit a bill (in a format determined by the lead agency) on a monthly basis by the 6th of the month for services in the previous month. The subcontractor will be reimbursed in the amount of $100 per client served and will submit documentation of service delivered with each invoice as itemized in Exhibit A attached. In addition, the subcontractor will conduct program evaluation both formal and informal as itemized in Exhibit B attached.

A failure to perform under this contract will result in the immediate termination of this agreement and may result in forfeiture of funds received. The parties agree to have disagreements heard by a professional arbiter.

This agreement may be terminated by either party with a three-month written notice in the case of all other reasons. Notices to either party are to be mailed via U.S. mail to:

Amber Smith, Executive Director	Ray Mellor, Executive Director
Geta Grant Agency	Boys and Girls Club of Grant City
1111 Grant Way	4444 Fun Street
Grant City, MA 22333	Grant City, MA 22333
Signatures of one Executive Director	Date:_____
Signature of the second Executive Director	Date:_____

Finishing Touches

Documents to Be Attached

If possible, create a cover page for each document you attach such as financial statements, board of directors, organizational chart, IRS designation, and so on. This will make it easier for you to insure that you have attached everything the funder is requesting. Use the application checklist, if one is provided, to insure all attachments are in place.

Send it off with a flourish, take a nice long breath, and celebrate! It is complete; it is *off* to the *funder*! (Make sure you send the proposal with delivery receipt required if mailed through the U.S. Postal Service or obtain a tracking receipt from overnight delivery services. If possible, when the grantor's address is nearby, hand deliver the proposal to the funder and obtain a receipt.

And, now the wait begins. Remember, 50% of the proposals funded are resubmissions that were denied the first time. This statement is not made to discourage you, but, rather, to ground you a bit in the reality of the process. Up to 90% of proposals submitted to the federal government get denied at the first submission. Because this is a highly competitive business, grant writers learn not to take rejection personally. In fact, too much personal investment in the proposal can work to your disadvantage, as you may lose the objectivity needed to negotiate the proposal, make modifications, or even learn from mistakes.

If you do receive a rejection notice, take a couple of days before you approach the funder. Once you are rebalanced, (and have the frustration out of your voice) see if you can obtain a copy of the scoring of your proposal to see how it ranked in relation to others and to learn what may need to be improved or changed in another submission. Remember, we all have had proposals turned down. The proposals that lose are not necessarily bad ideas or bad proposals. They may not have met the funder's idea for a project, they may have not demonstrated the need that other areas can demonstrate, or they may be ahead of their time. When this happens to you, take a breath, shake it off, and climb back into the writer's seat!

Notification of Funding

Let's hope you receive notice of funding and the application has been approved. It is gratifying and wonderful to get this notification! Obviously, it is time to celebrate the promise of funding for a project. The agency executive director is usually the designated contact, and he or she will be contacted first. If, by chance, the grant writer learns first, contact the agency executive director and the project director before saying anything to anyone else. Let the announcement be made by an agency official.

The grant writer may be asked to make the phone calls to the partner agencies to let them know the project is funded. You may also want to prepare a press release and give it to the project director to submit to local newspapers so the community will know about the funding. This press release and a brief letter should also go to local legislators and the city council so that they can learn of the good your agency is doing through the new funding.

Prepare a thorough, but short, summary of the project to be given to board members or others in the community, especially any agencies or organizations who will benefit from this funding. You also want to prepare a Project Tracking Timeline (see below) indicating the project reporting and evaluation timelines and, if the grant writer is a regular employee of the nonprofit, it helps to create a tickler file of the reporting dates for grants, renewal dates, or other important deadlines. The computer's calendar can be used for this function by inputting dates into the future that need to be remembered. It will be very helpful to send out reminders to the project director of upcoming due dates.

Sample Project Tracking Form

Project Reporting Timeline for: Healthy Families

Project Director: Mary Smith

Funder: **Contact Name:**   **Phone:**

Address: **Email:**   **Fax:**

Funding Period: January through December 20xx

Reports Due on: April 10, July 10, October 10, and Final Report due January 10, 20xx

Evaluation:

- Pre- and post-tests for all participants to demonstrate knowledge gain
- Documentation of client participation using sign-in sheets
- Completion of GPRA forms on 50% of all clients
- Follow-up phone calls to determine client satisfaction on 20% of all clients

Billing:

Submitted monthly in arrears of service delivery using funder-developed forms.

Finally, you may want to keep a professional notebook of your own that outlines the grants you have written and the outcome of each. Grant writers will often give a total amount of funding they have obtained in their careers, saying, "I've obtained 1.2 million dollars in grant aid in support of programs for the homeless."

We sincerely hope that this book helps you have a successful grant-writing effort and, if appropriate, a successful grant-writing career. The community needs you!

Appendix A

Estimating Time

In this section, we have provided for the beginning grant writer an illustration of the process involved in calculating a staff person's time expenditure on a project. Let's suppose that Geta Clinic wants to provide an AIDS-prevention education program in the county schools. The objective states:

Three thousand (3,000) at-risk youth will increase their knowledge by 30% on HIV transmission and risk-reduction behaviors by June 30, 20xx.

The implementation activities, with staff responsibilities include the following:

1. Relationship established with schools (Project Director, Community Educator)

2. Education programs developed and scheduled (Community Educator, Administrative Assistant).

3. Parent Orientation Nights planned and conducted (Community Educator)

4. Two, 1-hour educational presentations provided in the student's regular classroom on the nature of HIV transmission, risky behaviors, decision-making skills, and assertiveness training (Community Educator)

5. Student evaluation using pre- and post-test to indicate knowledge change (Community Educator and Administrative Assistant)

Someone without any knowledge about community education might say:

Okay, this is simple. An average class size would be 25. Divide 3,000 youths by 25 per class to find out how many actual classes you need; that equals 120 classes. Since the educator will spend 2 hours in each class, that is a total of 240 teaching hours. If I divide 240 hours by 8 hours/day, then I need a community educator for 30 days.

The above reasoning process is *faulty* for a number of reasons. What factors need to be considered when implementing a community education program for Geta Clinic? The following discussion will provide an example of the kind of "thinking through" process needed to develop a more realistic estimate of the time it will take.

Access to the Community

Has the clinic ever provided educational programs in the schools? How much time will it take to develop the necessary relationships with the schools to gain access? How much time will be spent scheduling programs? How much time in community relations to develop the network? Will the sensitive nature of the topic have an impact on this development time by making it even more difficult to gain access to the classroom?

Service Preparation, Evaluation, and Documentation

How much preparation will be required to provide the educational program in addition to the direct teaching time? Will the educator need to write the curriculum? Will he or she also need to evaluate the program's effectiveness? Grade the evaluation exams? Maintain other program records? Develop handouts for classroom use?

Geographic Location

How many sites can be reached in a day? Consider the traffic patterns, distance, and climate, for example.

Ethnic, Cultural, Linguistic Considerations

Will the clinic need educators from different ethnic backgrounds? What languages will need to be spoken? Written? Is a special knowledge required to work with this specific population(s), and, if so, how much time will it take for the educator to acquire that?

Human Capability

Finally, consider what is humanly possible to require of a community educator in terms of actual teaching within a given day or week. The energy required in the classroom when the speaker is an "outsider" is considerably greater than when the audience is familiar with the person. Once the program has gained access to the schools, perhaps one 2-hour presentation per day is all you can reasonably expect someone to do and maintain enthusiasm in the process.

Putting It All Together

Now it is time to recalculate the amount of time required from the educational staff. A full-time employee works 2,080 hours per year. You have determined that the educator will need to spend time developing relationships with the schools. You might estimate that it will take approximately 8 hours of contact time on the phone and in person per school that you want to reach. There are 50 high schools and, therefore, to contact each high school, it would entail about *400 hours.*

Then, you calculate that it will take the educator approximately 2 to 3 weeks full time to review the materials that are available and to plan the curriculum. If portions of the curriculum need to be written or evaluation tools developed, it would take, you estimate, about one month or *174 hours.*

We already know that the teacher will spend 240 hours in the classroom. He or she will go to 120 different classes and let's say you estimate that it will take 30 minutes travel time each way, so that is another 120 hours in traveling time. So the time spent in classroom presentations and travel time totals *360 hours.*

You have also calculated that it will take the educator approximately 1 hour per class to handle the evaluation component, which equates to another *120 hours.* You also want the educator to have a minimum of 10 hours per month to improve his or her skills and knowledge, to update records, attend an in-service training or other meetings, and to respond to correspondence, which adds up to another *120 hours* for a total of *240 hours* associated with conducting the evaluation.

Finally, let's add the fact that, due to the sensitive nature of the materials to be addressed in the classroom, the community educator will also need to be involved in making a presentation at "Parent's Night" so that they may review materials and ask questions. This will require 2 hours at 50 schools for another *100 hours* plus the 1 hour travel time for *50 hours.* There will be networking with other community groups, involvement on task forces or committees, which take another 5 hours per month or *60 hours* per year. That's a total of *210 hours.*

The total number of hours involved in the community educator's work comes to *1,384 hours for the project year.* There are 2,080 hours in a work year. Some planners will tell you that once you have made your best time estimate, it is wise to add an **additional 25%** or, in this case, an additional **520 hours.** The reasoning behind this is that things will always take more time than you think and there will inevitably be delays. In the case of the Geta Clinic, it appears that it would be wise to hire a full-time educator (100%) to reach 3,000 teens with an AIDS prevention program.

In the way that we have conceptualized the job now, the educator will spend the first 4 to 5 months preparing to teach and making contacts with the schools, and the remaining 7 months of the project year providing the actual service. The factors we have included in calculating the amount of time an educator would spend to reach 3,000 teens should follow the implementation activities fairly closely. These calculations will also be needed as you determine the cost of the project. Often, as the true extent of time and effort needed are revealed, the implementation activities or the objectives may need to be modified.

Appendix B
Funding Resource Information

L isted below are common sources of information on funding resources that you might find helpful. This is a selective listing; for a more complete picture of funding opportunities, you can consult your local library, or contact one of the following organizations/websites.

Grants.gov

Provides a website for federal agencies to post funding opportunities and to assist grantees to find and apply for them.

Web address: http:/www.grants.gov

Grants, Etc.

The University of Michigan's website offers access to funding sources, in-kind resources, electronic journals, how-to guides, and other valuable resources.

Web address: http://www.ssw.umich.edu/resources/index2.html?collection =grants

The Grantsmanship Center

An organization that has an extensive inventory of funding information, publishes a newspaper for grant-seeking organizations, conducts national training on proposal writing and other areas of human service administration, conducts workshops on grant writing, offers consulting services, and offers a grant database.

Mailing Address: P.O. Box 17220, Los Angeles, CA 90017
Physical Address: 350 South Bixel St., Suite 110, Los Angeles, CA 90017
Web Address: http://www.tgci.com

The Foundation Center

An independent, national service organization established by foundations to provide an authoritative source of information on private philanthropic giving; publishes various directories and guides on foundations; and has established a national network of reference collections through local and university libraries, community foundations, and nonprofit organizations.
Mailing Address: 79 Fifth Avenue/16th Street, New York, NY 10003
Web Address: http://www.fdncenter.org

Internet Addresses of Selected Federal and State Funders

Catalog of Federal Domestic Assistance: www.cfda.gov
Grants.Gov: www.grants.gov
U.S. Department of Housing and Urban Development Grants:
    www.hud.gov/grants
National Institutes of Health (NIH): www.nih.gov
Substance Abuse and Mental Health Services Administration:
    www.samhsa.gov
U.S. Department of Health and Human Services: www.dhhs.gov
U.S. Department of Education: www.ed.gov

Major Publications

Annual Register of Grant Support. Information Today, Inc., 143 Old
    Marlton Pike, Medford, NJ 08055
Catalog of Federal Domestic Assistance. Superintendent of Documents,
    U.S. Government Printing Office, 732 North Capitol Street, NW,
    Washington, DC 20402
Federal Grants and Contracts Weekly. John Wiley and Sons, Inc., 111
    River Street, Hoboken, NJ 07030
Federal Register. Superintendent of Documents, U.S. Government Printing
    Office, 732 North Capitol Street, NW, Washington, DC 20402
Publications of the Foundation Center, 79 Fifth Avenue/16th Street, New
    York, NY 10003
Foundation Directory
Foundation Directory Supplements
Foundation Grants to Individuals
National Directory of Corporate Giving

The Foundation Center's Guide to Proposal Writing
The Grantseeker's Guide to Winning Proposals
Foundation Fundamentals

Computerized Searches and Databases

There are a number of computerized search services available that provide funding resource information. The advantage of such databases is that they can subdivide and index the funding information into a range of subjects and categories (e.g., by subject, by geographic area). The costs can vary, and some of the information overlaps in the different databases. Check your local university library for more information about services. (Library tip: If you are no longer a student and want to use a university library, check to see if they have a "Friends of the Library" program. You may be able to join for a reasonable amount per year through this fundraising arm of the library.)

Dialog's *Information Retrieval Service* is among the largest databases covering a broad range of topics. Among the funding-related databases in the service are the following:

- Federal Register Abstracts
- Federal Research in Progress
- Foundation Directory
- Foundation Grants Index

Computerized searches are also useful for readily identifying literature and data for the needs/problem statement section of the proposal. One might find journal articles or other educational resources at such sites as

- PsycINFO database
- ERIC
- EBSCOhost database: Social Science Abstracts
- Medline/PubMed
- Nexis Lexis

Online Journals and Newsletters

The Chronicle of Philanthropy: http://www.philanthropy.com
Philanthropy News Digest: http://philanthropynewsdigest.org
Grantsmanship Center Magazine: http://www.tgci.com/centered-magazine-archive

Appendix C

Proposal Sections

The Letter of Intent

The purpose of the letter of intent is to inform the funder as to what your proposed project is about, in the hope that the funder will be interested in the program and allow you to submit a full proposal. You should enclose enough detail so that the funder can see the details of the project, as well as the rationale for the project. It is a good idea to show this letter to a friend and ask them if the proposed project is clear and if it sounds interesting and exciting to them. Try to keep the letter to 1 to 2 pages or to the length requested by the funder.

Sample Letter of Intent (on agency letterhead)

Dear Funder:

The XYZ Agency is pleased to apply for funding under Application PO71652: Funding Community Health Initiatives in Hispanic Populations. XYZ Agency has 26 years of experience providing health programs and services to the Hispanic/Latino population in Whatchamacallit County, PA. Local-level research indicates that our 580,000 member population is most in need of prevention services in diabetes and hypertension, as these two disease areas represent 80% of deaths to adults caused primarily by obesity. Food preferences and activity levels are mostly set in childhood, and, accordingly, our project focuses on children and young adults in an effort to prevent these conditions. Project AYUDA brings a unique strategy to bear: (1) activity offerings meet cultural preferences such as soccer, folkloric dancing, and bike riding; (2) cooking classes where the youth cook and serve their families reduced calorie versions of family favorites; and (3) educational information on diabetes and heart disease. Four cohorts of 30 children and young adults in this project will meet after school, 5 days a week, for 6 weeks over the course of this 9-month (school year) project.

At the completion of the project, we expect that the children and young adults who were overweight at the beginning will have lost weight and will have increased exercise by 20% over the previous level. We also expect the participants and their families to increase their knowledge of diabetes and heart disease prevention by 20%. In addition, we will evaluate the programs capacity to change behaviors long-term and expect that the families will adopt the new, reduced-calorie recipes for daily use in their homes. The total budget request is $209,827.

The Cover Letter

A letter of transmittal on agency stationery, signed by the appropriate organizational official, should convey interest in the funder's mandate and mission and state how the project fits within these mandates. The letter should be brief (usually 1 page); it should indicate the agency's board approval of the proposal; the contact person, with telephone number; the amount requested; and the willingness to respond to any questions about the project. Also, include a paragraph that summarizes the project as well.

Remember that the letter is often the first contact between the agency requesting funds and the prospective funder. Set a tone of professionalism and competency.

Sample Cover Letter (on agency letterhead)

Dear Mr./Ms. Funding Officer (if you know it) or Dear Formal Business Name of the Funding Agency (Dear U. S. Department of Health):

The XYZ Agency is pleased to submit this application for funding under PA714532 School and Community Safety. The project, called AYUDA, means help in Spanish and represents the culmination of 6 years of collaborative efforts between the XYZ Agency, the Putnam School District, and the Boys and Girls Clubs of Putnam County. We are alarmed that up to 80% of our local program population will develop Type 2 diabetes and/or heart disease by the age of 50 (Grant County Health Statistics—2014). Our partnership (with the XYZ Agency serving as lead agency) has crafted a project using local data and "best practices" known to positively impact the health issues we target to improve the health outcomes in our community.

Project AYUDA will offer culturally appropriate and exciting counseling, educational, health services, and sports and activities through afterschool and evening programs at the school and the Boys and Girls Club. The program will improve the health status of 120 children, ages 10 to 13, and their families (a total of at least 400 persons). In addition, it will reach broadly into the Hispanic community with information and pubic events designed to improve the knowledge and activity level of the community as a whole. We will measure the programs success with using pre- and post-testing of educational attainment, health status measures, and reports of exercise behavioral change. The total cost of the project is $209,827.

We are happy to respond to any questions you may have and look forward to hearing from you.

Sincerely,

Executive Director	Executive Director	Superintendent
XYZ Agency	Boys and Girls Clubs	Putnam School District
(888) 899–0987	(888) 899–6789	(888) 567–8765

The Title and Title Page

Develop a title that reflects the major goal(s) of the project. While one may develop a "catchy" title, its meaning should be readily understood by the reviewers. A descriptive subtitle might be used to clarify. Avoid long titles, or ones that are used too often by other projects.

A title page usually accompanies the proposal. Federal and state agencies will often provide the face sheets necessary. While there is no standard format for the title page, the following is typical:

Project Title

Name of the Agency Submitting Grant

Agency Address

Name of Prospective Funder

Project begin and end dates

Amount requested

Sample Title Page

Agency Name: XYZ Agency   Date: November 15, 20xx

Project ID: PA714532 School and Community Safety

Project Name: AYUDA

Fiscal Agency: XYZ Agency   Contact: Ann Martinez, Executive Director

Address: 2172 Main Street, Whatchamacallit, PA 87765

Phone: (888) 333-9876   Email: am@xyzagency.org   Fax: (888) 333-9877

Submitted to: United States Department of Education

Anticipated Project Term: October 1, 2017 to September 30, 2018

Request: $209,827

About the Proposal Abstract

The abstract is usually written after the other sections, since it gives an overview of the entire project. Unless the funder provides other instructions or forms, the abstract is typically no longer than 1 page. The abstract is used by the funder to screen the proposal for appropriateness in light of their funding objectives. A glance at the abstract also assists staff in disseminating the document to the proper review committees or funding offices. Once a proposal is funded, the abstract is often used by funders to convey to the public their funding decisions and activities.

Although it is sometimes hurriedly written at the end, care and attention should be given to its content. This is not the proposal introduction, but, rather, it is a complete summary of the entire project. As such, the abstract should parallel the major sections of the proposal. An abstract will typically

1. identify the agency requesting the funds,

2. describe the target population,

3. summarize the needs/problem statement highlighting data which show the magnitude or extent of the problem,

4. provide a synopsis of the project objectives including goals and objectives,

5. highlight the evaluation plan and the expected outcomes or results of the project, and

6. provide an "amount requested" figure.

Sample Project Abstract (Max 100 Words)

Project AYUDA by XYZ Agency, the Putnam School District, and Boys and Girls Clubs will reduce precursors to Type 2 diabetes and heart disease in 400 persons in a high-risk, Hispanic community. (Persons in this low-income community have an 80% greater risk of Type 2 diabetes and heart disease than higher income areas.) The program targets youth, ages 10 to 13, and their parents with health services/assessments, counseling, nutrition planning, and afterschool activities. Parents meet monthly to encourage outdoor activity. Participants will improve health by 25% (weight reduction, activity, access to health care) by project end. Request is $209,827.

Appendix D
Additional Information

---

1. Determining Percentage Change in Evaluation

The easiest type of indicator measure is knowledge change because you can give a pretest before the intervention to determine the amount of knowledge a person currently has, and then give a post-test to determine the amount of knowledge the person has at the end of the service. In other words, you measure the knowledge of the individual at the start and again at the end. Hopefully, the person had a higher score (knew more) at the end than they did at the start of the service or program!

Here is a simple formula to determine percentage of change: (1) subtract the starting value from the ending value, (2) divide that number by the starting number, and (3) multiply by 100 to convert that rate to a percentage. Example: A student scored 82 points on the pretest and 92 points on the post-test. 92–82 = 10. 10/82 = 0.1219 x 100 = 12.19% or simply 12%.)

2. Sample Size Determination Using Krejcie and Morgan Table

Small-Sample Techniques (1960). *The NEA Research Bulletin,* Vol. 38.

N	S	N	S	N	S
10	10	220	140	1200	291
15	14	230	144	1300	297
20	19	240	148	1400	302
25	24	250	152	1500	306
30	28	260	155	1600	310
35	32	270	159	1700	313
40	36	280	162	1800	317
45	40	290	165	1900	320
50	44	300	169	2000	322
55	48	320	175	2200	327
60	52	340	181	2400	331
65	56	360	186	2600	335
70	59	380	191	2800	338
75	63	400	196	3000	341
80	66	420	201	3500	346
85	70	440	205	4000	351
90	73	460	210	4500	354
95	76	480	214	5000	357
100	80	500	217	6000	361
110	86	550	226	7000	364
120	92	600	234	8000	367
130	97	650	242	9000	368
140	103	700	248	10000	370
150	108	750	254	15000	375
160	113	800	260	20000	377
170	118	850	265	30000	379
180	123	900	269	40000	380
190	127	950	274	50000	381
200	132	1000	278	75000	382
210	136	1100	285	1000000	384

Note: N is population size. S is sample size.

References

Krejcie, R. V., & Morgan, D. W. (1970). Determining sample size for research activities. *Educational and Psychological Measurement, 30*(3), 607–610.

(Found on the KENPRO web site www.kenpro.org which addresses issues of project management.)

3. Program Design and Evaluation Case Study

So that you might see how an evaluation plan becomes integrated into the program plan, let's begin with a hypothetical discussion: Let's say that my overall program goal is to prevent unintended adolescent pregnancy. I want to design a teen pregnancy prevention program for young adolescents. I am aware of the fact that this is a developmental period in which peers have a significant influence upon each other. As I read the professional literature, I find that social learning theory is one way to understand peer pressure and social norms. I select a curriculum for my program that is developed on the principles of social learning theory and I design my program to include traditional classroom instruction, a teen theater component, (the peer-to-peer aspect of social learning theory), a parent education component to improve parent and child communication, and a community advocacy component to address social norms promulgated through advertising and the media (again, a component of social learning theory). (Each of these program components will be written as measurable objectives.)

Then, as I am reading the program evaluation literature, I find the types of activities that have been used in the past in such programs, and their success in reaching their goals. Suppose that I learn that the classroom educational component is more effective when provided by college-age adults as compared to teens or older adults, and, consequently, I choose to design my educational intervention using college-age students. In this case, I can be said to be following *best practices* in that I am combining a sound theoretical orientation with a proven service delivery plan. I am now most likely to succeed.

4. Government Requirements of GPRA

The following description itemizes what the agency needs to provide to the federal government to comply with the Government Performance Results Act of 1993 from the OMB. The website at Whitehouse.gov states:

Sec. 306. Strategic plans

(a) No later than September 30, 1997, the head of each agency shall submit to the Director of the Office of Management and Budget and to the Congress a strategic plan for program activities. Such plan shall contain—*"(1) a comprehensive mission statement covering the major functions and operations of the agency;*
(2) general goals and objectives, including outcome-related goals and objectives, for the major functions and operations of the agency;
(3) a description of how the goals and objectives are to be achieved, including a description of the operational processes, skills and technology, and the

human, capital, information, and other resources required to meet those goals and objectives;

(4) a description of how the performance goals included in the plan required by section 1115(a) of title 31 shall be related to the general goals and objectives in the strategic plan;

(5) an identification of those key factors external to the agency and beyond its control that could significantly affect the achievement of the general goals and objectives; and

(6) a description of the program evaluations used in establishing or revising general goals and objectives, with a schedule for future program evaluations.

(b) The strategic plan shall cover a period of not less than five years forward from the fiscal year in which it is submitted, and shall be updated and revised at least every three years.

5. Human Subjects Review Code of Regulations

From HHS.gov

Code of Federal Regulations
Title 45 Public Welfare

Section 46.101 To what does this policy apply?

(a) Except as provided in paragraph (b) of this section, this policy applies to all research involving human subjects conducted, supported, or otherwise subject to regulation by any federal department or agency which takes appropriate administrative action to make the policy applicable to such research. This includes research conducted by federal civilian employees or military personnel, except that each department or agency head may adopt such procedural modifications as may be appropriate from an administrative standpoint. It also includes research conducted, supported, or otherwise subject to regulation by the federal government outside the United States.

(1) Research that is conducted or supported by a federal department or agency, whether or not it is regulated as defined in §46.102, must comply with all sections of this policy.

(2) Research that is neither conducted nor supported by a federal department or agency but is subject to regulation as defined in §46.102(e) must be reviewed and approved, in compliance with §46.101, §46.102, and §46.107 through §46.117 of this policy, by an institutional review board (IRB) that operates in accordance with the pertinent requirements of this policy.

(b) Unless otherwise required by department or agency heads, research activities in which the only involvement of human subjects will be in one or more of the following categories are exempt from this policy:

(1) Research conducted in established or commonly accepted educational settings, involving normal educational practices, such as (i) research on

regular and special education instructional strategies, or (ii) research on the effectiveness of or the comparison among instructional techniques, curricula, or classroom management methods.

(2) Research involving the use of educational tests (cognitive, diagnostic, aptitude, achievement), survey procedures, interview procedures, or observation of public behavior, unless:

   (i) information obtained is recorded in such a manner that human subjects can be identified, directly or through identifiers linked to the subjects; and (ii) any disclosure of the human subjects' responses outside the research could reasonably place the subjects at risk of criminal or civil liability or be damaging to the subjects' financial standing, employability, or reputation.

(3) Research involving the use of educational tests (cognitive, diagnostic, aptitude, achievement), survey procedures, interview procedures, or observation of public behavior that is not exempt under paragraph (b)(2) of this section, if:

   (i) the human subjects are elected or appointed public officials or candidates for public office; or (ii) federal statute(s) require(s) without exception that the confidentiality of the personally identifiable information will be maintained throughout the research and thereafter.

(4) Research involving the collection or study of existing data, documents, records, pathological specimens, or diagnostic specimens, if these sources are publicly available or if the information is recorded by the investigator in such a manner that subjects cannot be identified, directly or through identifiers linked to the subjects.

(5) Research and demonstration projects which are conducted by or subject to the approval of department or agency heads, and which are designed to study, evaluate, or otherwise examine:

   (i) Public benefit or service programs; (ii) procedures for obtaining benefits or services under those programs; (iii) possible changes in or alternatives to those programs or procedures; or (iv) possible changes in methods or levels of payment for benefits or services under those programs.

(6) Taste and food quality evaluation and consumer acceptance studies, (i) if wholesome foods without additives are consumed; or (ii) if a food is consumed that contains a food ingredient at or below the level and for a use found to be safe, or agricultural chemical or environmental contaminant at or below the level found to be safe, by the Food and Drug Administration or approved by the Environmental Protection Agency or the Food Safety and Inspection Service of the U.S. Department of Agriculture.

(c) Department or agency heads retain final judgment as to whether a particular activity is covered by this policy.

(d) Department or agency heads may require that specific research activities or classes of research activities conducted, supported, or otherwise subject to regulation by the department or agency but not otherwise covered by this policy, comply with some or all of the requirements of this policy.

(e) Compliance with this policy requires compliance with pertinent federal laws or regulations which provide additional protections for human subjects.

(f) This policy does not affect any state or local laws or regulations which may otherwise be applicable and which provide additional protections for human subjects.

(g) This policy does not affect any foreign laws or regulations which may otherwise be applicable and which provide additional protections to human subjects of research.

(h) When research covered by this policy takes place in foreign countries, procedures normally followed in the foreign countries to protect human subjects may differ from those set forth in this policy. [An example is a foreign institution which complies with guidelines consistent with the World Medical Assembly Declaration (Declaration of Helsinki amended 1989) issued either by sovereign states or by an organization whose function for the protection of human research subjects is internationally recognized.] In these circumstances, if a department or agency head determines that the procedures prescribed by the institution afford protections that are at least equivalent to those provided in this policy, the department or agency head may approve the substitution of the foreign procedures in lieu of the procedural requirements provided in this policy. Except when otherwise required by statute, Executive Order, or the department or agency head, notices of these actions as they occur will be published in the FEDERAL REGISTER or will be otherwise published as provided in department or agency procedures.

(i) Unless otherwise required by law, department or agency heads may waive the applicability of some or all of the provisions of this policy to specific research activities or classes or research activities otherwise covered by this policy. Except when otherwise required by statute or Executive Order, the department or agency head shall forward advance notices of these actions to the Office for Human Research Protections, Department of Health and Human Services (HHS), or any successor office, and shall also publish them in the FEDERAL REGISTER or in such other manner as provided in department or agency procedures.[1]

---

[1]Institutions with HHS-approved assurances on file will abide by provisions of Title 45 CFR part 46 subparts A-D. Some of the other departments and agencies have incorporated all provisions of Title 45 CFR part 46 into their policies and procedures as well. However, the exemptions at 45 CFR 46.101(b) do not apply to research involving prisoners, subpart C. The exemption at 45 CFR 46.101(b)(2), for research involving survey or interview procedures or observation of public behavior, does not apply to research with children, subpart D, except for research involving observations of public behavior when the investigator(s) do not participate in the activities being observed.

6. Sample Photographic Release

(We provide this as a sample to you—develop a release using this format on agency letterhead and take it to an attorney prior to use.)

The Geta Grant agency is asking your permission to photograph, video, or audio record you and/or your children. We will use the photos, videos, or sound recordings in our brochures, newsletters, annual reports, or other printed or audio materials that we develop to advertise our services, report to our donors and community, and report to our funders. The agency may place these images in publications that we sell. **You (or your children) will receive no financial or program advantage by agreeing to participate in the photographs, videos, or audio recordings.**

We need your permission to use any photo, movie, or voice recording. When you sign below, you give us your permission.

_____	_____
Name	Date
_____	_____
Address	City and Zip
_____	_____
Phone	Email
_____	_____
Name of Minor Child	Your Permission (Sign here again)
_____	_____
Name of Minor Child	Your Permission (Sign here again)
_____	_____
Name of Minor Child	Your Permission (Sign here again)

7. Line-Item Budget Worksheet

Personnel	FTE	Monthly Range (FTE)	Monthly	Yearly
Executive Director				
Project Director				
Educator				
Therapist				
Admin Assistant				
Subtotal Personnel				
Benefits @ ___%				
Total Personnel				
Operating Expenses				
Communications				
Rent (___s.f. x ____per s.f.)				
Office Supplies				
Printing				
Program Materials				
Furniture/Fixtures				
Equipment Purchase (computer)				
Equipment Rental (copier)				
Program Liability Insurance				
Conference				
Mileage at _____				
Subtotal Operating				
Indirect at ___% Total Budget				
Grand Total				

References and Suggested Readings

American Red Cross. (2016). *Mission and values.* Retrieved from http://www
.redcross.org/about-us/who-we-are/mission-and-values

Bandura, A. (1986). *Social foundations of thought and action: A social cognitive theory.* Englewood Cliffs, NJ: Prentice Hall.

Brewer, E., Achilles, C., Fuhriman, J., & Hollingsworth, C. (2001). *Finding funding: Grantwriting from start to finish, including project management and Internet use* (4th ed.). Thousand Oaks, CA: Corwin.

Burke, M. A. (2002). *Simplified grantwriting.* Thousand Oaks, CA: Corwin.

Carr, C. E. (2015). *The nuts and bolts of grant writing.* Thousand Oaks, CA: Sage.

Diamond, H. (1998). A perfect union: Public-private partnerships can provide valuable services. *National Parks Forum, 40*(4).

Dictionary.com (n.d.). *Philanthropy.* Retrieved July 1, 2012, from http://dictionary
.reference.com/browse/philanthropy

Dluhy, M., & Kravitz, S. (1990). *Building coalitions in the human services.* Newbury Park, CA: Sage.

Foundation Directory Online: The Foundation Center, 79 Fifth Avenue/16th Street, New York, NY 10003-3076. (212) 620-4230 or http://www.FoundationCenter
.org

Gantt Chart. (n.d.). Retrieved May 21, 2016, from https://en.wikipedia.org/wiki/
Gantt_chart

Gardner, S. (1999). *Beyond collaboration to results: Hard choices in the future of services to children and families.* Fullerton: California State University, Center for Collaboration for Children.

GrantCraft: A service of the Foundation Center, 32 Old Slip, 24th Floor, New York, NY 10005-3500. http://www.grantcraft.org

Hatry, H. (1996). *Measuring program outcomes: A practical approach* (4th ed.). Alexandria, VA: United Way of America.

Internal Revenue Service. (2016, April 4, updated). Forms and publications. Retrieved from https://www.irs.gov/Forms-&-Pubs

Kenya Projects Organization, Macjo Arcade, Suite 15E, Next to Tuskys, Ongata Rongai, P.O. Box, 8076–00200, Nairobi http://www.KENPRO.org

Kettner, P. M., & Martin, L. L. (1987). *Purchase of service contracting.* Newbury Park, CA: Sage.

Kettner, P. M., & Martin, L. L. (1996). *Measuring the performance of human service programs.* Thousand Oaks, CA: Sage.

Kettner, P., Moroney R., & Martin, L. (2008). *Designing and managing programs: An effectiveness-based approach.* Thousand Oaks, CA: Sage.

Kiritz, N. J. (1980). *Program planning and proposal writing.* Los Angeles: The Grantsmanship Center.

Kniffel, A. (1995). Corporate sponsorship: The new direction in fundraising. *American Libraries, 26*(10), 1023–1026.

Knowlton, L., & Phillips, C. (2009). *The logic model guidebook: Better strategies for great results.* Thousand Oaks, CA: Sage.

Krejcie, R. V., & Morgan, D. W. (1970). Determining sample size for research activities. *Educational and Psychological Measurement, 30*(3), 607–610.

Lauffer, A. (1997). *Grants, etc—grant getting, contracting and fund-raising for nonprofits.* Thousand Oaks, CA: Sage.

Melaville, A. (1997). *A guide to selecting results and indicators: Implementing results-based budgeting.* Washington, DC: The Finance Project.

National Center for Charitable Statistics: The Urban Institute, 2100 M Street NW, 5th Floor, Washington, DC 20037. http://nccs.urban.org/statistics/quickfacts.cfm

Netting, F. E., & Williams, F. G. (1997). Is there an afterlife? How to move towards self-sufficiency when foundation dollars end. *Nonprofit Management & Leadership, 7*(3), 291–304.

Peterson, S. (2001). *The grantwriter's Internet companion.* Thousand Oaks, CA: Corwin.

Poor Law. (2012). In *Encyclopedia Britannica.* Retrieved from http://www.britannica.com/EBchecked/topic/469923/Poor-Law

Roth, J., Brooks-Gunn, J., Murray, L., & Foster, W. (1998). *Promoting healthy adolescents: Synthesis of youth development program evaluations. 8*(4), 423–459.

Ruskin, K., & Achilles, C. (1995). *Grantwriting, fundraising, and partnerships: Strategies that work!* Thousand Oaks, CA: Corwin.

Schaefer, M. (1987). *Implementing change in service programs.* Newbury Park, CA: Sage.

Schorr, L. (1995). *The case for shifting to results-based accountability.* Washington, DC: Center for the Study of Social Policy.

Schram, B. (1997). *Creating small scale social programs.* Thousand Oaks, CA: Sage.

Soriano, F. I. (1995). *Conducting needs assessments: A multidisciplinary approach.* Thousand Oaks, CA: Sage.

Sternberg, R. J. (2014). *Writing successful grant proposals from the top down and bottom up.* Thousand Oaks, CA: Sage.

Thayer, K. (2012, January 25). Hull House closing Friday. *Chicago Tribune*. Retrieved from http://articles.chicagotribune.com/2012-01-25/news/ct-met-hull-house-20120126_1_child-care-union-contract-employees

UC Berkeley Public Health Library: http://www.llib.berkeley.edu/PUBL/grans.html

U.S. Department of Health and Human Services Division of Grants. (2016). *Get ready for grants management*. Retrieved from http://www.hhs.gov/grants/grants/get-ready/index.html

Vinter, R. D., & Kish, R. K. (1984). *Budgeting for not-for-profit organizations*. New York: The Free Press.

Young, N., Gardner, S., & Coley, S. (1994). Getting to outcomes in integrated service delivery models. In *Making a difference: Moving to outcome-based accountability for comprehensive service reforms* (National Center on Service Integration Service Brief 7). Falls Church, VA: National Center for Service Integration.

Performance Indicators

The Accreditation Council on Services for People with Disabilities. (1993). *Outcome based performance measures: A procedures manual*. Towson, MD: Author.

Annie E. Casey Foundation. (2011). *Kids count data book: State profiles of child well-being*. Baltimore, MD: Annie E. Casey Foundation.

Conoley, J., & Impara, J. (1995). *Mental measurements yearbook*. Lincoln, NE: Buros Institute of Mental Measurements.

Department of Health and Human Services. (1995–1996). *Performance measurement in selected public health programs* (Regional Meeting Report). Washington, DC: Public Health Service.

Kumfer, K., Shur, G., Ross, J., Bunnell, K., Librett, J., & Millward, A. (1993). *Measurement in prevention: A manual on selecting and using instruments to evaluate prevention programs*. Washington, DC: Center for Substance Abuse Prevention, U.S. Department of Health and Human Services.

Touliatos, J., Perlmutter, B., & Straus, M. (1990). *Handbook of family measurement techniques*. Newbury Park, CA: Sage.

U.S. Department of Health and Human Services. (1994). *Assessing drug abuse among adolescents and adults: Standardized instruments* (Clinical Report Series). Rockville, MD: National Institute on Drug Abuse, Public Health Service.

Weiss, H., & Jacobs, F. (1988). *Evaluating family programs*. New York: Aldine de Gruyter.

Index

About the Authors

Soraya M. Coley is president of California State Polytechnic University (Cal Poly), Pomona. Prior to that, she served as provost and vice president for academic affairs at California State University, Bakersfield, and at Alliant International University, as well as dean of the College of Human Development and Community Service at California State University, Fullerton. She has nearly 30 years of higher education experience and has worked with nonprofits, community-based and civic organizations on program design, evaluation, and grant writing.

Cynthia A. Scheinberg has 23 years of senior administrative leadership in the nonprofit sector. She served as executive director of the Coalition for Children, Adolescents, and Parents (CCAP) in Orange, California; as senior vice president of clinical services for Anka Behavioral Health; and as executive director for New Connections, both in Concord, California. As such, she has successfully designed, written, and obtained federal, state, and foundation proposals. Now retired, she consults on grant writing and compliance issues. Her email address is: proposalwriting5thed@gmail.com.

SAGE was founded in 1965 by Sara Miller McCune to support the dissemination of usable knowledge by publishing innovative and high-quality research and teaching content. Today, we publish over 900 journals, including those of more than 400 learned societies, more than 800 new books per year, and a growing range of library products including archives, data, case studies, reports, and video. SAGE remains majority-owned by our founder, and after Sara's lifetime will become owned by a charitable trust that secures our continued independence.

Los Angeles | London | New Delhi | Singapore | Washington DC | Melbourne